Life and Times
on the Dale

Stories and Photographs of Silverdale

Barry Williams

CHURNET VALLEY BOOKS
Leek, Staffordshire: 01538 399033
Publishing Local History
Specialist Bookseller of Ornithology and Biography

© Barry Williams and Churnet Valley Books 1998

ISBN 1 897949 52 9

DEDICATION

For Stuart and Alistair, my beloved grandsons

ACKNOWLEDGEMENTS

I am indebted to the many people of Silverdale who have assisted me in bringing this book to publication. In particularly I am grateful to the following for their special help, valuable time and encouragement:

Graham Bebbington

Neil Collingwood

Brian Nixon

Graham Payne

Frank Procter

Anthony Roberts

In addition to the above I would like to thank:

Mrs Elsie Ashley OBE, Lilian Barlow, Brian Bonsall, Graham Bytheway, John Carnal, Glynn Edwards, Pearl Edwards, Margaret Furnival, Phillip Hollins, Councillor Bill Hughes, Mick Jones, David Lee, Alice Malkin, Cliff Rogers, Pauline Rogers, Paul Roper, Ralph and Brenda Rowley, Ivan Shipley, Lily Trotter, Graham Whittaker and Matthew Williams.

CONTENTS

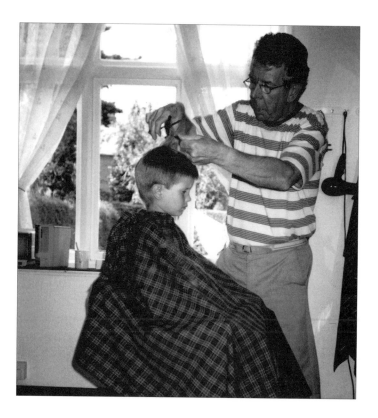

A General View of Silverdale, showing the colliery, coalyard and railway station. The old Brighton Cottages
and St Luke's Church are in the background.

Rural aspect of Silverdale - originally part of Birchall's farm, it is now the site of the
Municipal Golf Course. New housing development in the foreground and Kent's Lane Colliery in the centre.
The farm fiel ds in the background are pre-open cast mining. *Graham Bebbington collection*

INTRODUCTION

As I grew up, Silverdale village was a lovely mining villagecontaining a wealth of knowledge, mainly in the mining community. Many people of renown, locally, nationally and internationally have come from this village.

At the beginning of the book you will find a map of the village I have drawn, showing all the streets and the details I can remember of the 87 shops which were occupied and trading when I was a youngster. Silverdale was a very self-contained place with every need catered for. There were twenty-seven public houses, three working men's clubs and three off licences - in those days called beer-offs, presumably because people fetched beer in jugs and bottles to drink at home.

For entertainment there were several choirs from the various Chapels, a great community pastime. The arrival of the Roxy cinema was a turning point in my young life, and it was always full. The Youth Club concert party was renowned for its talented artists, most of whom of course also sang in the choirs. They used to give two concerts a year, always packed to the door.

Religion played a large part in family life in Silverdale and the village had four Methodist chapels, Wesleyan in Newcastle Street, Free Church in High Street, Primitive also in High Street, and Bethel in Church Street, as well as St Luke's Church of England in Church Street, the Congregational in Victoria Street, the Elim Pentecostal in Albert Street -which was a very small place - and the Roman Catholic Church again in High Street. I will refer to some of the wonderful characters and their families who ran these places.

Silverdale has always been a Labour stronghold both in local and national politics. I have realised what a lot of changes have taken place in the past fifty years as I try to recall my memories in this book. I have deliberately not spent much time on the colliery as this has been written about many times, but I do hope to revive a few memories of Kent's Lane where my own father worked for many years. The bad news is that the colliery will now close again for good in December 1998.

During the re-development of Silverdale Shopping Centre a lot of controversy arose about knocking down the old shops and what damage this would do to the community. The council proposed to build 23 shops and 21 maisonettes in the centre of the village. The council agreed to meet the shopkeepers to discuss the matter. After much debate, work finally started in 1969 and a nice scheme was eventually built and opened with all the shops being taken. The shops now (1998) are not doing so well and quite a few are empty with the large supermarkets taking away their trade. Stupid acts of vandalism also cause a problems for the shops and residents.

Hairdressing has been a very rewarding experience for me and all these stories and memories come from meeting people from all walks of life in my trade. I have written down these nostalgic stories because I feel that they should be put on paper before the people who tell them are gone and forgotten. Along with the stories are a collection of photographs most of which have been lent to me by customers. I hope they tell some of the many other stories of 'Life on the Dale'.

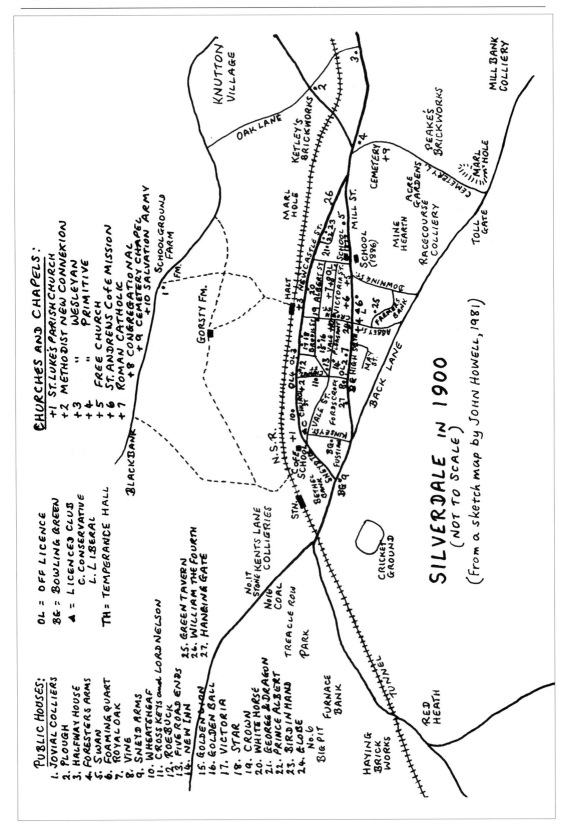

SILVERDALE IN 1900
(NOT TO SCALE)
(From a sketch map by JOHN HOWELL, 1981)

Chapter One
THE AUTHOR - BARRY WILLIAMS

I was born in Silverdale March 28th 1935 and lived at my parents' shop on the corner of Crown Street and Newcastle Street. I started to school at five attending Silverdale Infants' School and transferring at eight to the Junior School. Mr Fred Cork was our headmaster, very strict but always very fair. He certainly was an expert with the cane which was used a great deal at that time. "Six of his best", as he called them, on your hands certainly hurt. Not many went back for more after their first caning. Mr Faulkner, Mr Whalley, Miss Balance, Miss Hinchcoe, are all teachers I recall with great pleasure.

My parents were very friendly with Mr and Mrs Redfern of Gorsty Farm which was reached by going up the Jolly's entry - it is still there now - and up the fields to their farm. I spent many years of my young life on this farm, sometimes sleeping there for days because my parents knew that I was very safe with the Redfern family. I wore clogs on the farm and knew every place that hens layed their eggs, so off I would go with my small wheelbarrow and collect them in hundreds for Mr Redfern to sell on his milk round.

I had ten bantam hens of my own, which produced a delicious small egg when they laid - I would eat two or three at one meal with bread and butter. I also looked after the farm pigs, young calves, and at eight years of age I could milk cows by hand easily. At ten years old, in the autumn ploughing season I was allowed to lead the large carthorse by hand up and down the furrows, not easy when you got to the end of the furrow and had to turn around and go back the other way, especially with me about four feet high and a horse twice the size. But he was so gentle, it was no problem.

The pictures of me on Redfern's Farm were sent by my mother to my brother Sid during the War. Sid was in the Navy on HMS Wheatland, a destroyer. Sid was 16 years older than me so he loved to be kept in touch with what I was up to. These pictures were sent around the World to Sid and my parents never knew until he came home from the War whether he had received them or not. When he came home Sid said that it was these photos and others like them which kept his spirits up.

During the War double summer time was introduced to allow farmers more daylight hours. This meant it was light until almost midnight, as well as being light enough to work again by 4.00 am. At harvest time during August and September, quite a few people from Silverdale village would come to help out getting the corn harvest in. Every available cart, truck, in fact anything which could carry the corn, would be used to try to get it under cover before rain. If it got soaked it took ages to dry. The first tractor was a Fordson Major with no tyres to cushion the bumps up and down the banks of the farm fields. The back wheels had large spikes to that it would not slip or skid but what a hard ride! I often think back to the two hardworking but friendly men who worked on the farm at that time, Jim Lewis and Ern Nicklin, who lived at the cottage at the rear of the farm. Both left and eventually went to work at Silverdale Colliery.

Another event on the farm was potato picking week in November. Mr Redfern would go to the local senior school to get permission for about twenty boys, aged thirteen to fourteen, to have a week off school to hand pick potatoes directly off the field. Imagine this in November; rain, sludge, and back breaking work, but my pals and myself always managed to get a place being well in with Mr Redfern. One thing was certain, you slept very well that week. When we got paid on Friday it was well worth it plus the bonus of a week off school.

Time was approaching for me to think about getting a job. When I left school I was approached by Alf Harrison the hairdresser in Church Street to take up an apprenticeship for five years. He said that Joe Hough the newsagent had recommended me and would I like to join him. I must admit the thought horrified me. The idea of being a hairdresser just did not appeal after enjoying farming all these years. My mother and father asked me to try the job for six months; if I did they would buy me the new bike I so badly wanted from Mickey Barratt's bike shop in Newcastle Street. I gave in and started in March 1951 and here we are in 1999 and still hairdressing forty-seven years on!

In 1985 at fifty years of age I took up running and in 1987 I ran my first of twelve marathons over thirteen years, raising over £8000 for various charities through my customers sponsoring me. In June 1990 my daughter Karen gave birth on holiday in Torquay to a son Stuart who was just under 2 lbs in weight. He was transferred to Exeter Intensive Care Baby Unit where he was critically ill. He remained here for nine weeks fighting for his life. But gradually he began to improve and with wonderful doctors, nurses, and family help, he was eventually transferred by ambulance to Billinge Hospital near to Wigan where Karen and her husband Mark live. He had five weeks in their hospital before at last at 14 weeks old he was taken home. We were so grateful that he had pulled through I decided to run the Potteries Marathon for the North Staffs Intensive Care Baby Unit and it raised £875 for their unit.

Stuart was born with a cleft lip and palate to add to his problems. In 1990 he had plastic surgery on his lip and in 1991 he had surgery on his palate, both with excellent results. In 1996 I ran the Potteries Marathon for C.L.A.P.A. and this time we raised £1,075 - all through the wonderful support of my customers.

The picture here shows Stuart running the last few hundred yards at the finish of the marathon at Trentham Gardens with his Grandpa.

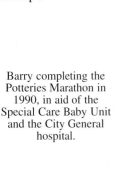

Barry completing the Potteries Marathon in 1990, in aid of the Special Care Baby Unit and the City General hospital.

Egg collecting time, and below, in the far stockyard looking after a newborn calf and a kitten.

Harry Redfern, the farmer's son.
with Barry, seen here with Chum,
the dog. Harry is holding the farm
guard dog, who lived his life
outdoors in a large kennel.

School pals.
Standing:
John Wade and Cliff Sims
Sitting:
Barry Williams and Paddy Thornton

My father Bill Williams and I with our horse Nellie

Three of us from Silverdale Boys' Club spent a week's
holiday cycling around Wales,
Cliff Sims, Graham Glover and Barry Williams

A very young Barry Williams with Jewel,
Redfern's working horse in 1944.

Jolly's Entry - a popular short cut to the Colliery Football Ground and Redfern's fields; also to Knutton village. The railway line to Silverdale station and colliery ran across the top.

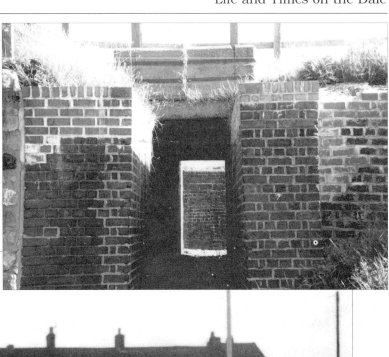

Church Street/Crown Bank. This is where I was born, on the corner of Crown Street. The place is now a dental surgery

Glynn and Howard Edwards, cousins, in their younger days.

Silverdale Junior School, now demolished.

Infants' school, youth club and evening centre. Now used as social and educational centre.

Silverdale Junior school football team, late 1950s.

Silverdale County Primary 1930s

A little before my time - Silverdale Junior School c1920. Note the overhead gas lights.

Not many smiles - Monday morning?

Silverdale Junior School 1951. Headmaster Mr Fred Holland.

Silverdale Junior school classes, about 1950

The school prefects of Knutton Secondary Modern School 1949.. Twelve of these came from Silverdale.

Knutton Secondary School Prefects 1950, with headmaster Mr Fred Beech.
Fifteen members of this group came from Silverdale.

Due to subsidence problems, the children are moving from the Mill Street site to their new school on the Racecourse

School's on the move

Silverdale Primary School Christmas Fair, 1970

HIGH STREET, SILVERDALE

My first hairdressing salon, which opened in 1956 at the junction of
High Street and Sneyd Terrace.

Photograph taken at Beech Caves. On Sunday morning cycle rides, ten or a dozen of us would set off round the
country lanes. Hardly any of us had any gears on our bikes, not like today with 21 gears! Pictured on this
photograph in July 1949 left to right; Bert Tanner, Harry Brereton, Gordon Forrester, Bob Davies, Cliff Sims,
Roy Morall, Back Row; Roy Ashley (smoking), Peter Beswick, Gordon Johnson and yours truly Barry Williams.

Author's parents and sister-in-law outside Buckingham Palace

Two good pals -both overmen at
Silverdale Colliery.
Jack Ikins and my father, mother and
sister-in-law, enjoying a day out at
Blackpool.

Hair styling competition, Manchester. My model was
David Talbot, who worked as a fitter at Silverdale
Colliery. We gained sixth place.

Three members of Michelin's Athletic Club, who
between them raised £600 for the Antony Nolan
Bone Marrow Appeal when they volunteered to have
their heads shaved by Barry.

Below:Boys Club Concert Party, 1950s, with barber
Ken Ellams and his customers, left to right:
Ron Tanner, Stan Philips, Tony Lawton, Boyce
Fisher and Terry Ellams.

Barry and Audrey Williams present a cheque for £825 to Guide Dogs for the Blind, September 1989.

Presenting a cheque for £875 to the Baby Care Unit at the City General Hospital, August 1991.

1995. Barry, his wife Audrey, daughter and son in law Karen and Mark, and grandsons Stuart and Alistair.

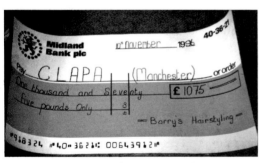

Potteries Marathon 1996 and cheque for CLAPA
(Cleft Lip and Palate Association)

Daughter Karen, on the occasion of her graduation
from Chester College, October 1982

Chapter Two
SPORT 'ON THE DALE'

Cricketers from Silverdale

Joe Ankers

A local lad who was a brilliant batsman in the same era as Charlie Rushton. Joe was born on the Dale and played all his cricket for Silverdale. It has been said many times that Joe could easily have gone on to county cricket. He was a bachelor living with his mother who suffered poor health so he would not leave home under any circumstances. His main hobby was pigeon racing and the stories go that often Joe got out when batting if the pigeons were returning to their cotes. He would have one eye on the ball and the other in the sky trying to see if his pigeons had won their race.

John Charles Cooper

John Charles Cooper was a senior clerk with Silverdale colliery. He lived in Sneyd Terrace and so had just a short walk to work across the way from his house. He was an excellent number three batsman and played as a professional for Lancashire at his peak. He could be seen every Tuesday night at the net practice and always passing on good advice to any younger players.

Charles "Charlie" Rushton

Another Silverdale Colliery wages' clerk who played for Staffordshire and apparently could have gone on and done much better - but he had a very good job, which meant a lot then. So he stayed at the colliery until he retired.

Sam and Jack Norcup

Two good fast-bowling brothers, who both played for Silverdale and Staffordshire. Jack was a very steady bowler, quite fast and able to bowl for long spells. Sam was a 'very fast', big, muscular chap who played for Staffordshire regularly and had a trial with Lancashire but was turned down, because he had a slight round arm action. Sam moved on to Porthill as a professional and ended his cricketing days there. He worked in Silverdale Colliery and was in charge of the Check Weigh office.

George Shaw

George Shaw was a very good run-getting opening batsmen who opened the batting for years for Silverdale. He also played for Staffordshire. He worked at the colliery in the wages office.

Jack Shaw

An excellent batsman, medium-paced bowler and a great wicket-keeper. He moved from Staffordshire to become a professional cricketer and groundsman in Llandudno. He eventually came back to the area and worked at Silverdale Colliery as a mechanical fitter. He played for several other clubs before he retired.

Tom Whittaker

A Silverdale lad born and bred, Tom was a left arm bowler, quite fast, and an opening batsman. His bowling action and curving run-up looked quite strange but was very effective. His batting was excellent too, which resulted in him playing for Staffordshire and he eventually left Silverdale to play professionally for Kidsgrove, then later reverting back to play for Longton CC. After retiring from cricket, he carried on a very successful career as an architect.

Graham Bytheway

Another Silverdale lad who was an excellent opening bat for years, Graham was known for his lovely, smooth batting style. He was the captain of the North Staffs League Team. When he eventually stopped playing cricket, he continued as the treasurer of the club until he handed over to Brian Nixon.

Silverdale Colliery Football Team late 1950s
Back row: Doug Rogers, Brian Amphlett, Eric Ward, Cliff Rogers, Albert Wagstaffe
Front row: Russell Dumbell, Arthur Dumbell, Graham Pearce, Boyce Fisher, Ron Jarrett

Silverdale Second Team, 1955
Back row: Billy Hill, Fred Beech, Terry Brookes, Harry Redfern, Bernard Ward, Frank Edwards, Brian Nixon
Front row: Ken Bytheway, Terry Ellams, Eddie Bytheway, Bill Brown

Badminton Club
L to R: Barry Williams, Dinah Hollins, Joyce White, Mike Jones, Beryl Redfern, Harry Redfern

Morleys Radio Team, 1954 Half Holiday League
Back Row: F Birch, Vince Stanley, Don Collings, Fred Donaldson, John Latham, Stan Cotton, Fred Dean
Front Row: John Howells, Brian Ross, Barry Williams, Dennis Bloor, Ken Ross

Brian Nixon

A very good Silverdale cricketer, Brian was an excellent batsman, playing shots all round the wicket, and he was a brilliant fielder, especially close to the wicket. When he watches cricket now and sees close-in fielders wearing crash helmets, he must think lucky me, never to have been seriously injured. Brian also represented the League Team.

Mick Jones

Another Silverdale lad who was an excellent left hand bat and also a medium pace bowler. He worked his way from second team to captain of the first team. Unfortunately a car accident led to an operation to remove a disc from his back. He played for many years after, but never quite reached his previous standard. He never misses a match these days watching his son Steve who also is a very talented cricketer and plays in the Silverdale first team.

Silverdale Footballers

Ian Moores

Born in Silverdale, the middle boy of three, with Robert the eldest and Nigel the youngest. A sad thing hit the family when the boys were very young and their father Harry died suddenly, leaving their mum Phyllis to bring them up on her own - and what an excellent job she did of it.

The three went to Silverdale Primary School, where Ian's talent began to show at football. Leaving this school he went to the Edward Orme School in Gallowstree Lane where he improved and was chosen for the Staffordshire County Schools team. When he left school Ian was signed by Tony Waddington for Stoke City, and by this time he was 6' 3" and a really big lad.

His position was centre forward and he certainly was very intimidating to play against. Ian's only problem was he would not hurt a fly he was such a nice lad; he was never really aggressive. He eventually arrived in Stoke City First Team and was playing alongside Jimmy Greenhoff who taught him a lot at this time. Ian began to score goals and Stoke were doing well.

One morning Ian had a real surprise. Don Revie, the England manager, called him for the under 23 team. Sports commentators and newspaper sportswriters were forecasting an excellent future for Ian. This particular day Ian had promised to come to my hairdressers shop to have his photograph taken and give autographs to 10 eight year old boys who were beginning to hero worship him. The boys and their parents arrived at the shop before 6.30 pm. I had to warn them that Ian, owing to the special excitement of this day, might forget to come. But 6.30 pm arrived and Ian was dead on time, and he spent a full hour with these kids. The photograph shows Ian with Michael Grocott on his knee. Michael is now twenty-eight. I always remember Ian for that little session with those children.

In the meantime things at Stoke City were changing, with a little unrest in the camp. Jimmy Greenhoff was sold to Manchester United, so Ian's striking partner had gone. Things got a little frustrating for Ian as he was still learning his trade. Suddenly Tony Waddington sold him to Tottenham Hotspur, which in one way was a wonderful move for him. He improved and still scored goals but he never really settled with Spurs. He moved onto Leyton Orient and after about four years there he moved back North to play for Bolton. He ended his career in Cyprus where he was very popular and was once voted one of the top three players ever to play football in Cyprus.

One often wonders how good he would have been playing alongside Jimmy Greenhoff for a couple more seasons. Ian was always a nice lad, smart, clean and a credit to the way his mum Phyllis had brought him up. Sadly this story has a very tragic ending with Ian getting cancer and passing away in January 1998. He was married to Anne and lived in Biddulph. They had two sons, Richard and Michael, who were his best pals. Richard plays for Knypersley Vic's Youth Team. Ian managed this team until November 1997 when he became too poorly to take his place on the touchline.

Ian Moores in action.
At the outset of his career with Stoke, Ian played with stars like Peter Shilton, Geoff Hurst, Alan Hudson, Jimmy Robertson and Jimmy Greenhoff

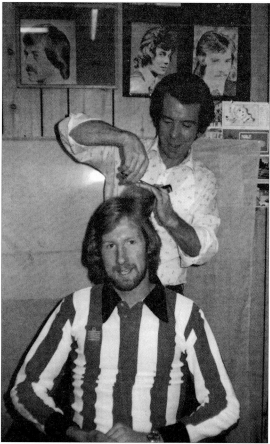

Ian Moores had this trim prior to playing in the England Under 23 Squad

Hundreds mourn former Stoke City star

MORE than 350 people attended the funeral of former Stoke City star Ian

By Sentinel Reporter

He was a very ill man but he hung on for Richard's 16th birthday party with the family all around him. Ian's funeral was a celebration of his life and a footballer named Vince Yates gave the tribute speech which was brilliant. So many things he said made me think back on Ian's younger life. Ian's wife, Anne, and his sons, Phyllis his mum, and his brothers, must have been very proud of him. The three tributes to him in the Evening Sentinel by his old pals Alan Bloor, John Ritchie and Jimmy Greenhoff, show what a great lad he was.

But to finish this story on a happy note, I have very reliable information that a new Moores is on the way to football. Tom, Nigel's ten year old, is at Crewe School of Excellence showing lots of promise and scoring plenty of goals.

Ian Moores with Michael Grocott in my barber's seat

John Ridley

John was a very good midfield player who came from Park Site Estate. He passed his 11 plus examination to go to Wolstanton Grammar School. When he left Wolstanton he went to Sheffield University to study mathematics. In the meantime he signed for Port Vale and soon was playing in the first team. He travelled home most week-ends from Sheffield to play but still kept his first team place. John passed his maths degree and shortly after transferred to Leicester where he kept his first team place for years.

John was a lovely natural ball player and would have probably gone further but combining his academic career held him back a little. John has managed several successful local teams and still teaches mathematics in Stoke-on-Trent.

Harry Redfern

Harry played at centre-half or left-back. Hard as nails, never shirking a tackle, he signed for Stoke City after turning down several big named clubs. He played part-time at Stoke regularly in the reserves. Stoke wanted him to sign full-time but Harry was running his farm and did not dare to risk that in case he got injured. He left Stoke and played for Stafford Rangers part-time for years.

Billy Brayford

A right little character. He was with Port Vale for a few seasons and was a brilliant little inside-right. He shot with both feet and was a brilliant header of the ball. Bill decided not to go ahead with a football career and carried on to complete his apprenticeship in painting and decorating with Joseph Jones, builder. Many people felt that Bill should have carried on with football but once he had made his decision that was that.

Graham Whittaker

Graham left school at fifteen in1951 and joined Stoke City straight away. A big strong full-back or centre-half, Graham improved rapidly with professional coaching. He joined the R.A.F. at eighteen, and served two years playing football at a high standard for Fighter Command. Unfortunately Graham then received a nasty knee injury and was advised not to play again.

Keith Broomhall

Keith signed for Port Vale as an apprentice when Stanley Matthews was manager. Keith was playing very well and his team reached the semi-final of the F.A. Youth Cup, but he was injured and could not play. Keith's injury was a shaved hip bone, quite a nasty injury at that time, and it cost him his professional career.

John Bostock

John joined Port Vale with Keith Broomhall straight from school. Again a Stanley Matthews product, John always looked very classy and a brilliant passer of the ball, but John failed to make the grade and left Vale Park after two seasons.

Steven Jones

Steven went to Silverdale County Primary School and at the early age his football talent began to show. Just before he went to Clayton High School aged 11, he was invited to join Manchester City Junior School of excellence. He played there for two years but in the meantime Stoke City started a school of excellence so Steven moved there. He stayed for two years but was not asked to sign professional forms, and moved to Audley. Then Kidsgrove Athletic signed him as a part time professional and after two more years he was transferred to Leek Town F.C. This was a good move for Steve, he improved his game and was spotted by Stalybridge in the Vauxhall Conference. He signed for them and is still playing there as semi-professional today.

Alan Davies

Alan went to Silverdale County Primary, moving aged eleven to Senior School at Edward Orme School. Alan certainly seemed to be heading for an excellent career. At fifteen, still at school, he gained international caps for England He too joined Manchester City and signed full time professional forms at sixteen. He was kept on at Manchester but not making the grade he went to Southampton for trials and again did not quite make it. He now plays semi-professional for Burton Albion. Once again so near and yet so far from a dream career.

Silverdale Colliery FC

This was a very successful team who all worked at the Colliery and played together for seven or eight years at the end of the 1950s early 1960s. They were trained by Ray Harp, Jack Ryder and Ern Dimond and they won several league titles during the period, as well as the League Cup, the Mayor's Charity Cup and the NCB Collieries Trophy. They were part of the Silverdale Colliery Sports and Welfare Section and were very well supported by Vic Ankarat the Colliery manager at the the time who also played for the team.

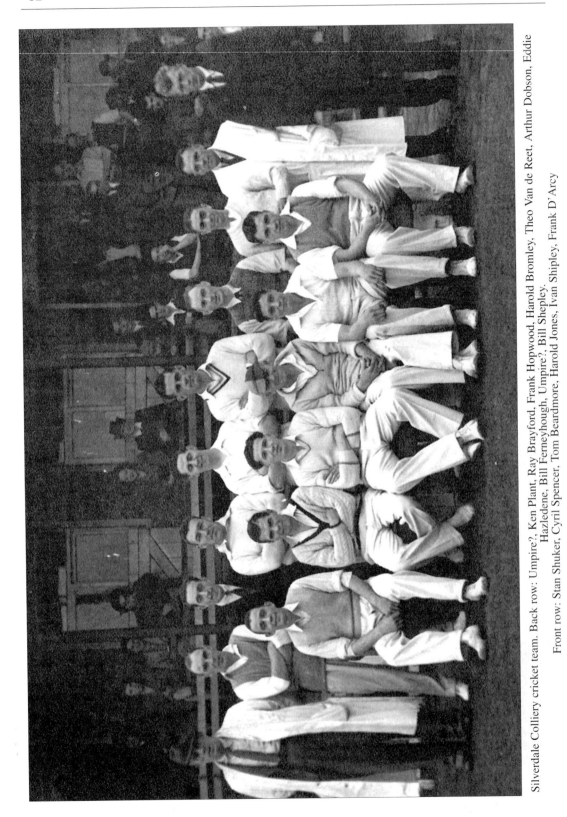

Silverdale Colliery cricket team. Back row: Umpire?, Ken Plant, Ray Brayford, Frank Hopwood, Harold Bromley, Theo Van de Reet, Arthur Dobson, Eddie Hazledene, Bill Ferneyhough, Umpire?, Bill Shepley.

Front row: Stan Shuker, Cyril Spencer, Tom Beardmore, Harold Jones, Ivan Shipley, Frank D'Arcy

George Shaw & Mick Jones walking
out to open the innings in 1959

Silverdale 1st Team late 1950s
Back row: Jack Myatt, Norman Stubbs, Arthur White, Eddie Bytheway, Tom Whittaker, Percy Procter
Front row: Billy Hill, Cliff Saunders, Fred Malkin, Sid Cooper, Charles Taylor (captain)

Silverdale 1st Team
Back row: Ern Griffiths, Jack Pearce, Cedric Spragg, Jack Shaw, Bernard Ward, Harry Redfern

Front row: Cec Lewellyn, Fred Malkin, George Shaw, Clifford Saunders, Bill Brayford (captain)

SILVERDALE CRICKET CLUB.
Hon. Secretary F. HOLROYD, 27, Abbey Street, Silverdale, Newcastle, Staffs.

Dear Sir,
    A Meeting of the Social / Ground / Management Committee will be held at ...... p.m. on ....

.... 196 .....

at the Conservative Club / Pavilion.

Agenda :—

Silverdale   Cricket   Club.

The Record first-wicket partnership in North Staffordshire League cricket was set up in 1935 by Joe Ankers and J. Bentley. of Silverdale C. C.   The Visitors, Stone, hit 243 for eight declared and left 133 minutes for Silverdale to knock off the runs. Ankers (not out 137) and Bentley (not out 100) passed the score with 27 minutes to spare.

(PRINTED 1958)

Silverdale
Cricket & Tennis
Club.

Active Members Subscription 12/6
Juniors 17 to 21 10/-
  „ 14 to 17 5/-

Season - 1949.

Silverdale Youth Club
Cricket Team: Winners of the Silverdale Cricket Club Knockout Competition, 1951
Back Row, Left to Right: Brian McGing, Ken Ellams, Bernard Ward, Stan Hall, Ron Tanner and Percy Procter.
Front Row, Left to Right: Terry Ellams, Barry Williams, Tom Whittaker (Capt.) Bill Brayford and Bob Davies

R to L:
Arthur Edwards, Jack Bossons, Bill Furmston, Albert Whalley, Len Peake, T Morrall, J Hanley - these cricket fans never missed a match - same time, same place every Saturday. This photograph was taken on 9th August 1963, during the North Staffordhire and District League match, when Silverdale defeated Michelin.

For these folk, Bank holiday meant cricket. They are pictured watching the North Staffordshire and District League (Senior Section) match in which Silverdale defeated Michelin.

Silverdale C.C. 1st team
Back Row: Mick Jones, David Bytheway, J. Pearce, Frank Procter, Percy Procter, Harry Redfern, Sid Cooper,
        Ern Griffiths, Fred Malkin
Front Row: Jack Shaw, Clifford Saunders (captain), George Shaw

Tea Ladies, 1947, Ladies' Pavilion
Mrs Berry with Avril, Mrs Lowe with Peter, Mrs Pointon with Maureen, Mrs Griffiths with Peter,
Mrs Thompson with Sylvia, Mrs Coomber, Mrs Enoch Procter with nephew David,
Mrs Bytheway with David, Mrs Malkin witth Robert

Spectators at a Friendly Match
Back row: Mrs Roy Barratt, Mrs Jack Norcup, Mrs Frank Procter
Front row: Mrs Bill Ferneyhough, Mrs Billy Hill, Mrs Jeff Morton, Mrs Fred Malkin,
Robert Malkin, Barbara Hand

1956 Cricket Champions
Back row: Bernard Ward, Gordon Birchall, Terry Ellams
Middle: Harry Brough, Billy Hill, Ern Griffiths, Harry Redfern
Front row: Fred Malkin, Frank Procter, Clifford Saunders, George Shaw, Eddie Bytheway, Bill Brayford

Silverdale Cricket Club

Knutton Secondary Modern Football Team Schools Champions, 1950
There are eighteen boys in the picture, fifteen from Silverdale and three from Knutton.
Front Row, Left to Right: Brian Rowley, John Wade, Barry Williams (Author), Graham Whittaker, John Viggars, John Davies and Ron Rowley
Middle Row, Left to Right: Reg Poole, Mickey Gannon, Joe Gallagher, Joe Kane, Arthur "Sugar" Massey, Dennis Rowley, Boyce Fisher, Ken "Tusher" Wood and John Johnson
Back Row, Left to Right: Arthur Cooper, Alf Dale (Sports Teacher) and Tony "Tut" Lawton

Moss United, with Fred Fisher's son Roger standing third left on the back row. He still runs his father's business, Frederick Fisher Electrics.

Silverdale Junior School Football Team, 1946-47
Back row: Mr Faulkner, Keith Street, Mr F Holland, Headmaster, Mr Tunnicliffe
Middle: John Bagguley, Keith Street, Brian Rowley, Jack Sanders, Mike Jones, Brian Bostock
Front row: Eric Ward, Keith Birchall, John Wade, Arnold Meakin, John Johnson

Boys Club team 1955 at Bourneville for Inter Boys Clubs Tournament
Back Row L to R: Boyce Fisher, Tony Lawton, Ted Ward, Cliff Rogers, Peter Deakin, Don Bourne, John Davies
Front Row L to R: Barry Bloomfield, John Tryner, Eric Rowley, Terry Ryan

Bowls at Silverdale Conservative Club
Back Row L to R: Albert Myatt, Fred Fisher, Reg Sutton, Roy Williams, Harry Rowe, Jack Bossons
Front Row L to R: Len Ford, Boyce Fisher, Joe Hough, Fred Malkin, Jack Lovatt.

Colliery Football Club taken outside colliery baths.
Back: Ray Harp, Russell Dumbell, Cliff Rogers, Brian Amphlett, Albert Wagstaff, Ray Hall
Front: Jack Ryder, Vic Ankaret, Boyce Fisher, Doug Rogers, Eric Ward, Graham Pearce, Arthur Dumbell

Colliery Football Club early 1960s
Albert Wagstaff, Graham Pearce, Boyce Fisher, Arthur Dumbell, Dave Rogers, Cliff Rogers, Russell Dumbell,
Ron Jarrett, with the League President presenting the trophy to Eric Ward.

Colliery Football Club
Russell Dumbell, Cliff Rogers, Vic Ankaret, Brian Amphlett, Cliff Weston, Colin Whittaker, Alf Whitehouse,
Graham Pearce, Eric Ward, Micky Gray, Bill Wilkinson, D. Wagstaff, Ray Harp, Frank Lee, Matthew Redfern

Colliery Football Club, League Cup winners early 1960s
Back: Russell Dumbell, Eric Ward
Middle: Albert Wagstaff, Brian Amphlett, Cliff Rogers, Ron Jarrett, ?referee
Front: Arthur Dumbell, Doug Rogers, Graham Pearce, Pat Conolly, Joe Matthews

Daleian Singers Conductor Glynn Edwards receives the trophy following another triumph at the Newcastle Music Festival

Cup of cheer - choir takes top honours at major competition

EVENING SENTINEL, Monday, September 21st, 1970

High standard at Daleian music concert

The Daleian Singers go from strength-to-strength. Their sucesses in the competition field were reflected in the standard of singing heard at their anual concert in the Queen's Hall, Burslem, last night.

Choir enjoys a notable success

A CHOIR hit the right note when it took part in Newcastle Music Festival and went home with a top trophy.

Chapter Three
ENTERTAINMENT 'ON THE DALE'

The Daleian Singers

The choir owes its origin to a group of choristers from the Silverdale Methodist Chapel who canvassed and recruited a limited number of experienced singers. They called themselves the Daleians, to reflect their geographical connection. The inaugural rehearsal of this Methodist inspired choral group took place at the Vine Inn in Silverdale.

Over the years the choir built up an enviable reputation as competitors in the Festival arena (seven appearances in the Final at the prestigious Blackpool Festival) and established themselves as one of the best small choirs in the country. Their successes include nine wins at the local Newcastle festival followed by first prizes at Blackpool (2), Bournville, Buxton, Southport, Tamworth, Pontrhydfendigaid and Minsterley (3 in succession).

Despite their Festival successes the Daleians have always regarded themselves first and foremost as entertainers. They have toured the Lakes on five occasions, given concerts in Cornwall, Yorkshire and Lancashire and a celebrity concert on Llandudno Pier. The choir have also been very active in North Staffordshire organising celebrity concerts at the Queens Theatre Burslem and the Victoria Hall, and local venues often in support of local and national charities. They have introduced many new singers to the public, as well as featuring established performers from the world of opera including international singers Stuart Burrows, Ann Dawson and Patricia Leonard of D'Oyly Carte.

The choir continually recruits new members from the Potteries and beyond. At one time two members travelled from as far afield as Walsall and Shrewsbury!

Festivals apart the choir have achieved many other firsts! The Daleians were the first local choir to hold their annual concert at the Victoria Hall. The first to discard traditional "penguin suits" in favour of smart blazers and the first to perform live on Radio Stoke. In the early days BBC Radio Stoke signed off their evening programme with a Daleian rendition of "Close Thine Eyes" by I. Reese Davies. The Daleians feature on a BBC recording of "Songs of Praise" one of a series of special recordings produced to celebrate the 50th Anniversary of the BBC.

The choir have produced their own records based on live concert performances.and recorded by Colin Clowes. From 1958 to 1990 the choir's annual subscription remained at £1 - yet another Daleian record! The multi-talented Daleians have fielded a useful cricket team and, as you would expect, a very competitive football XI. There is first class entertainment at every annual dinner - pantomimes, old-time music hall, instrumental music by the Maharishi and his Transcendental Band and a Daleian version of maypole and horn dancing.

Unfortunately there are a few grey and white heads among the choir and an injection of young blood is urgently called for. Newcomers are soon made to feel at home at our rehearsal room at the Orme Centre in Newcastle and enjoy a comradeship which is special to male voice choirs along with the keen but friendly rivalry which exists between the various sections of the choir.

One word of warning - newcomers will inevitably be regaled with tales of the glory days - as they have been for the last 20 years! The Daleians have enjoyed a long and distinguished history.

Silverdale Roxy Cinema

This is where the main attraction was on Saturday afternoons at 1.00pm - the '2d rush' was a queue hundreds of yards long waiting to see the Saturday cowboy film which started at 1.30pm.

Ken Pico, who was the manager, was very proud of his cinema and would have no fooling around. He employed 'Skinner' Wilson, a large, round and miserable man, with instructions "Don't let any idiots in". It was very upsetting to us kids when you paid your 2d and then got thrown out as soon as you had paid. Certain lads were always thrown out for bad behaviour but even parents did not argue with 'Skinner' - what he said was the last word!

Just before the film started 'Skinner' would walk on to the stage, with his red uniform and cap shining in the spotlight, to warn about noise and bad behaviour. Some lads sneaked pea-shooters in and would pepper him when he was trying to speak. It was comical to see them bouncing off his hard hat. He would give it up as a bad job and let the film start. When the film had finished you would see all the lads running around smacking their bottoms as if they were on horses and firing guns with their two fingers out. What pleasure they had from the 2d rush!

Another thing the Roxy did was to have a late film night on Saturdays for those who had their own shops and were open late - the show started at about 10pm - which again showed the great community spirit on the village. When the cinema was refurbished with new posh seats they put in four rows of double seats at the back which were very popular with courting couples and were always snapped up first.

Spooner's Dance Hall

This was between the Roxy cinema and the Royal Oak pub and originally owned by Mr and Mrs Spooner. Mrs Lowe ran the dancing and it was always packed out. They were all locals from Silverdale or nearby. The idea was to have a couple of dances and then into the Oak for a few drinks, and then back for a dance or two - and so on.

When the American troops arrived - and remember there were 700 of them based at Keele - some started to turn up at Spooners, and you can imagine the problems this brought about. The Yanks had plenty of money, cigarettes, chewing gum, nylons and so on, and it was soon pretty obvious who the girls were going to go for. The local lads couldn't stand them and fights soon broke out. But the girls certainly loved them!

Spooners closed soon after the War and in 1951 was bought by Syd Perkin and Edna Duffield, two of the best ballroom dancers in the world. They formed a dancing school which was soon very busy, with people coming from all over England for private lessons. The dance hall, open seven nights a week, proved very successful.

The school closed about 1970 when Syd and Edna moved to Newcastle to bigger and better premises. 'Spooners' was demolished as part of the site of the new and refurbished centre of Silverdale.

Silverdale Youth Club Concert Party

Every year there was a concert put on by the Youth Club, with ages ranging from 14 to 21. Boys and girls put on the shows with the experienced help of Fred Payne, Reg Brayford, Peter Deakin, Mick Whitehurst and Bert Tanner, who were the brains behind them. There was often a cast of 40 which needed a lot of organising but the shows were very professional because we had some fine singing voices and brilliant actors. Held in Silverdale Primary School in Mill Street for four nights in January, they were always completely sold out.

I suppose the most outstanding was Ralph Procter a schools education officer who was always very quiet and reserved. Ralph ran the Youth Club on two nights per week with the help of Margaret Hubbard. During rehearsals for the concerts Ralph completely changed character and was brilliant, very lively and comical, and the star of the show. His female impersonation was hilarious, the audience always wanted more. Others were Alice Harrison and Margaret Dunn both sopranos, and Thelma Taylor and her brother Gerald; both had lovely voices.

Syd Perkin Dancing school and dancing teachers.
Syd Perkin fourth from right, front row.

Syd Perkin and Edna Duffield.

The Great Van Buren

Fred Yoxall was the owner of a hardware store in the High Street but was to become one of the world's finest illusionists. He was described as a 21st century miracle man.

His first job as a boy was as an apprentice cabinet maker and he started to make his first props. Fred's wife Connie was his assistant for 23 years. By 1960 Fred had topped the bill in many famous theatres and played on the same bill as Jimmy James, David Nixon, Windsor Davies, Mike Yarwood, Ken Dodd, Paul Daniels, Vince Hill and Roy Castle - and many more.

Fred devised and built all his own illusions. His most famous trick was the vanishing motor-cycle and Fred was the only person in the world to perform this feat. He bought the bike in Ipswich and brought it to Silverdale to build his illusion. The Magic Circle heard of the trick and they wanted him to demonstrate at a large show in London. The trick really caught the imagination of the public and shortly afterwards the BBC filmed the illusion. It earned him international acclaim and he had the honour of being invited to the World Congress of Magic in Brussels, where he performed this wonderful illusion in the middle of the Grand Palace, filmed by TV crews from all over the world.

His special memory was meeting the Duke of Edinburgh who said to him, "I am unsure whether to shake your hand in case I go up in a puff of smoke". Fred's son Andrew is beginning to make a name for himself in show business and says about his own future, "It's got to be show business."

Van Buren and son - a proud moment when Andrew begins to exhibit his father's talent.

Van Buren performing the Vanishing Motor-Cycle Trick. This feat took him all over the world and made him a truly international illusionist.

1952 - Boys' Club Concert Party. Always the star of the show, Ralph Proctor shaking hands with the Mayoress, Mrs Bond, who had been to see the show.

Boys' Club Concert Party

Daleian Ladies at wedding of Dawn Furnival and Greg Warrilow 1985.

Silverdale Male Voice Choir, 1926

Dr Talbot presenting the darts awards in 1959

The Bush. Recently refurbished and opens all day serving food.

The Vine Inn, renowned for its beer, this is where Joe Steadman and Michael Donovan drank - see the Joe Steadman story.

The Crown - an excellent pub, very traditional and well supported. For many years it had its own bowling green, but this has long since gone.

The Sneyd Arms. It has now been modernised and renamed The Bush.

Chapter Four
PUBS ON SILVERDALE

SNEYD ARMS	WILLIAM THE FOURTH	ROE BUCK
HANGING GATE	BIRD IN HAND	WHEATSHEAF
VINE	PRINCE ALBERT	LORD NELSON
GREEN TAVERN	GEORGE AND DRAGON	CROSS KEYS
FOAMING QUART	WHITE HORSE	ROYAL KEYS
FORRESTERS ARMS	CROWN	ROYAL OAK
(CORNER PIN)	BOWLING GREEN	GLOBE
HALFWAY HOUSE	STAR	FIVE ROAD ENDS
SWAN	GOLDEN BALL	CONSERVATIVE CLUB
PLOUGH	GOLDEN LION	

Old Jovial Collier's Pub and Johnson's Clay Cricket Club

Johnson's Clay Cricket Club had a lovely little cricket ground and pavilion at the back of Redfern's Farm. They played in the old Stone League. It was a lovely little pitch, if a bit bumpy on the odd occasion. Harry Redfern, myself and Graham Bytheway turned out if they were short of players.

At the back of this cricket ground there was the old Jovial Collier's Pub which was run by Johnny Johnson and his wife, opening part time. Mrs. Johnson was housekeeper to the local priest on Silverdale for many years. When the cricket matches finished the players would go to Johnny's Pub and drink his very strong beer straight from the barrel. Johnny's takings would be boosted by these games and it was said that he hated the winters, because he had no cricketers to use his pub - it was not worth opening for. Eventually the pub was demolished and it carried on for a while as a smallholding, before being swallowed up in the opencast mining site.

The Star Inn, Church Street

This pub was run by Mrs Lily Woodcock who was a lovely, quiet lady. Her hair was always up in a bun on top of her head, and she always looked the same over the number of years that I knew her. The 'Silverdale White Star' football team was run from her pub; on Saturday afternoon in the backyard of the pub their would be about twenty buckets of cold water, so that when the players came back from the match, they could have a wash in the freezing water and then run into an outbuilding to get dried and dressed. When ready, they would go into the pub where Mrs Woodcock had lovely hot cups of tea and sandwiches waiting for them. After the War they changed the name of the team from the 'Silverdale White Star' to the 'Silverdale Ex Service' football club. This carried on for many years, still with the help of Mrs Woodcock.

The Swan Pub, Mill Street

This pub at one time was owned by Gertie Gitana the world famous music hall artiste and apparently her mother lived there for a few years. It was a large pub and always popular for a good sing song night out. One customer was Dixie Dean and his pals and local girls who were always up for a good night out. One story is that when the carpets wore out in the Swan he offered to tarmac the floors at a cheap rate - this being Dixie's profession of course.

The Swan had the first petrol pump on Silverdale. It had to be hand pumped, hard work for Paddy Darcy the landlord especially when he had a queue of cars. One day a chap called for petrol in a Rolls Royce, jumped out of the car and said to Paddy, "Fill it up please", and dashed in to use the toilet. In his haste he left the engine running and when he came out Paddy said to him, "Can you please turn your engine off sir, it is using it up faster than I can put it in. Paddy Darcy was one of three brothers. He ran the Swan and worked at the colliery, his brother Tom ran a grocery shop at the top of Sneyd Terrace, and another brother ran a small shop on the corner of Downing St and High St.

Royal Oak, another busy pub, patronised by dancers at Spooners Dance Hall which was next door down a small alleyway.

Right: The Roebuck, Church Street

Below: The Halfway House, Silverdale Road.

Chapter Five
CHARACTERS AND EVENTS

Harry White

Harry was a small man who was born with no roof in his mouth, so he had a very bad speech defect. He was a bright little chap who worked full time at the post office in Newcastle. He also had a large double fronted shop in Church Street which he opened in the afternoons and evenings seven days a week. He never married so he could do as he pleased.

He sold everything - toys, sweets, tobacco, cigarettes, stationery - anything that would sell, Harry sold it! At this time all men used to wear shirts that needed a collar stud. Harry sold these at threepence a time. One gentleman went in one day to buy one but Harry had run out. In a flash, Harry took out his own collar stud and sold it to the gentleman for one penny.

A lot of the local lads took advantage of Harry and would go into his shop in a group and steal things. One day as the firework season was approaching some lads went in and stole some fireworks and going out of the door some of them fell from under a lad's jacket on to the floor. Harry, ever helpful, said to the lad, "Hey Johnny you are dropping your fireworks", and gave him a bag to put them in - he thought he had brought them somewhere else.

There was always a funny smell in Harry's shop which no one could put a name to, but you never stayed in Harry's shop for long. He also had a passion for Durber's custard tarts and when he bought them he would say, "A tuppenny tustard tut in two please," - he could not say his 'c's.

Besides being a shopkeeper, Harry was a postman during the War and after, based at Newcastle with his post round on Silverdale. He was very dedicated and everything was done strictly to the letter! In those days on Silverdale the kids were given a film show once a week. The kids would look for Harry coming with his post bag and would ask him if he was carrying the reels of film. Harry would not tell the kids anything so they would follow him on his round until he came to the house where they were delivered. The owner would come to the door to sign for them and as soon as the kids saw him take the reels off Harry they would start cheering and running down the street shouting "the films are here, the films are here". People said that Harry never cottoned on as to how the children knew that the films had arrived - never once did he ever tell anyone what was in his bag.

Joe Steadman

Joe ran a Sunday-only newsagent business in Church Street. In those days no other newsagent was allowed to sell Sunday newspapers. He must have employed a dozen or more boys to deliver, each with a little wooden truck because they had such a lot of papers to deliver on the village.

His other thriving round was to Keele Hall - now Keele University - which at this time housed about seven hundred American troops. He delivered magazines and newspapers and had a wonderful line in contraceptives in which he was the main supplier. He would get supplies of sweets, chocolates, nylons and chewing gum in return. The Americans thought the world of Joe!

The Vine pub was renowned for its strong beer and Joe having plenty of spare time in the week would spend it drinking in the Vine. When I was a young apprentice many a time I had to cross the street to help Joe back to his shop. Joe's wife died after a short illness and Joe began to spend more and more time in the Vine. He befriended a little Irish man by the name of Michael Donovan who lived in Knutton Miners Hostel. The trouble was that Michael liked drinking as much as Joe did so they used to go on real benders. He eventually moved into the shop to live with Joe. The business was sold to Joe's nephew but Joe was allowed to live there. One morning Michael told a friend that he could not waken Joe - he was dead, and Michael was devastated. After a short while he was taken into care by the Little Sisters of the Poor in Cobridge.

Joe Steadman's Sunday only paper shop.

Michael Donovan in the Vine.

Bob Woodcock, baker

Bob Woodcock's Vase

Francis Stanyer Broad the owner of Silverdale Colliery and Forge presented this vase to his colliery manager Mr James Bostock for being an excellent servant in running his colliery. James Bostock was great-great-great-grandfather of Bob Woodcock and the vase was passed down to him. When Bob married he took the vase with him and when he died his wife sold it to Harry Sheldon a Silverdale antique dealer. When Mr. Sheldon died he left the vase to Newcastle Museum where it is today.

Church Street, 1947 - the worst winter for 50 years

Three foot of snow was on the ground, but the horse and milk float got through easily. All the houses in Church Street had sash windows, which are easy to open, you just lift them up. So when the milk arrived they opened their windows. The milkman, Mathew Redfern, served both sides of the road by having a long pole. He attached a small milk churn to the pole and then handed it to the customer, who would remove the churn, pour it into his or her own jug and pass it back.

Everyone gave the horse crusts and tit-bits. I can remember people throwing these bits on top of the snow, which was literally right under the horse's nose, it was so deep. On more open ground there were snowdrifts up to twenty feet deep. Village life was hardly upset because Silverdale was so self-contained. Can anyone imagine the chaos there would be today, with that amount of snow?

The Old Tin Church

This was run by Mr Ernest Diamond and his son Reg and was situated on the opposite side of the road from the chip shop, now Tupper's Fish Bar but originally known as 'Daniel's Chippy'.

Many happy hours were spent here by local young men, as there was a snooker table, some skittles and balls, and at the back another room where Mr Diamond and his son gave lessons in joinery. These two men were exceptionally good with boys who were interested in woodwork and with their guidance, many a nice piece of furniture and 'knick-knacks' were produced which the boys took home, quite proud of what they had achieved.

This building was of a corrugated iron construction, hence the Old Tin Church as it became affectionately known, and it housed a large coke-burning stove. Many a yarn was told as lads sat round, keeping nice and warm and exchanging stories and experiences.

The words "I'm bored, there's nothing to do" were never heard in the Old Tin Church. I dare say that many a person today can say thank you for the help and leadership given by Ernest and Reg Diamond.

Daniel's Chip Shop

After Youth Club a group of us would walk up from Mill Street to Daniel's Chip Shop on the corner of Earl Street. Some would buy chips and others would buy a bottle of Tizer, and we would share them between us, sitting outside on the shop window ledge. One of the first Vent-Axia fans was fitted to the window, and one of the lads noticed that this had been fitted the wrong way, and was blowing in instead of drawing out as it should have been. For a bit of fun we used to take the hard chip bits out of the bags, hold them up to the vent and 'flirt' them in - and people inside were bombarded by these bits. Mr Daniels would chase us but he never caught us.

Then one night we were caught out. We bought our chips from Rhode's chip shop and went back down to Daniel's to play our trick. Mr Daniels had opened the bedroom window and waited. As we stood beneath, he threw a bowl of water and mushy peas all over us. Obviously when we arrived home we were covered in this sticky mixture and our parents wanted to know what had happened. When we told them, we were in even more trouble and we had to go and apologise to Mr Daniels.

Shortly after the Vent-Axia was taken out and put back properly. Despite our mischievous behaviour, we were always made welcome at Daniel's Fish and Chip Shop.

The Okey Pokey Boys

Quite a lot of people still remember these Okey Pokey Boys and most remember that they were Jesse Myatt of Albert Street and George Talbot of Cherry Hill Halfway House. They sold ice cream for Mr Horace Lee, Reg Lee's father, who had his ice cream factory at Stonewall where North Staffs Caravans are now.

These lads rode a three-wheeled bike, with a large tub on the front. In those days the tubs were not refrigerated. They would set off from Stonewall carrying a handbell and when they arrived at their destination they would ring the bell and shout at the top of their voices "Okey Pokey One Penny A Lump". Apparently the response was immediate. The ladies ran out in to the street with basins to put the ice cream in. Then they would quickly go in to the house and put the ice cream into their icy cold pantry floor.

Jim McGing

Jim used to sit on the wooden seat at the bottom of the road leading up to the Cricket Ground, by the Bush Pub. He had had a nasty back injury at some time so could not work. He lived opposite this seat so he would spend hours each day talking to passers-by, to anyone who would talk. Bill Furmston and Albert Whalley were regulars with him. Jim had a lot of very funny sayings but the one I remember most was "if you have a cousin on the Council it is better than having a Father in Heaven".

Mathew Redfern

One very well remembered character of Silverdale was Mathew Redfern of Gorsty Farm. His farming land came right down behind his beloved Chapel, the Silverdale Wesleyan Methodist. He was well known as a local preacher which meant that he also preached some Sundays in Knutton, Madeley and Chesterton Chapels. He would get there by horse which was the only mode of transport in those days.

His main love in life was the Wesleyan, where he and his family would attend at eleven on a Sunday morning, at 2pm for Sunday School and the 6pm evening service. If you ask anyone who remembers him, the first thing they say is, can you remember when he used to chase the boys from playing football on the Jolly's playing fields on Sundays. The boys would put their jackets on the ground for goal posts and start to play when suddenly, Mathew would appear, running very fast towards them! Everyone would panic and start to run, quickly picking up their coats on the way. They would run for the Jolly's entry, which would take them into the safety of Silverdale's streets. His Sunday meant everything to him and he did not believe in playing football on the Sabbath.

One story told to me by his son Harry was about when the War finished in 1945 and the Sneyd family of Keele held a celebration day in the grounds of Keele Hall (now Keele University). One of the events was the 100 yards sprint, which Mathew entered in his 65th year. One can imagine it, athletes from all over Staffordshire arriving and getting changed into their running shorts, vests and shoes. Mathew arrived dressed in his black long breeches, boots and a shirt. When they all lined up for the race, he must have stood out like a sore thumb among the young men. Mathew won the first heat, to go through into the final, which he also won. He was such a fit man, working so hard for six days a week, but never on a Sunday, except for milking his cows.

He knew all his animals by name. He was a very kind person like that. He also delivered milk around Silverdale with his horse and float. On Saturday March 24th, 1938, he had an horrific accident on the level crossing at the Crown Street Crossing. Below is the headline from the Sentinel of what happened. What it does not tell is that his beloved Wesleyan Chapel was right by where the accident happened, so one could say that perhaps the Lord was with him, that day.

I never knew him to be ill at anytime throughout his life. But when he was 89 years old he became ill and died, peacefully at home on the farm, being looked after by his loving wife, daughter Joyce and son Harry and daughter-in-law Beryl. Matthew was a wonderful example of hard work,

Level Cross

PASSENGER TRAIN COLLIDES WITH MILK FLOAT

A Knutton Farmer's Narrow Escape

HORSE KILLED

Mathew Redfern and Barry Williams on the farm. This man's principle was 'never on a Sunday'.

The section of railway line where Matthew Redfern's horse was killed. The Wesleyan Chapel peaks out above the small building in the foreground.

clean living, and a wonderful Methodist. His son Harry and wife Beryl continued to work the farm but Silverdale Colliery were buying the odd field to expand and eventually a large expansion was planned. They made Harry an offer, to buy the farm and in 1978 Harry and Beryl reluctantly decided to sell and moved to Tibberton near Newport, where he and Beryl continue to live.

Reg Ikins

Reg, a bachelor, lived all his life in Victoria Street, and was employed by the Silverdale Cooperative Society until he was called up for military service. He joined the R.A.F. and rose to leading aircraft man, serving in India, Burma and Java. While out there he began to take an interest in the tea companies and invested in five of them.

When he came home he did not return to the Coop but went to work for the Ministry of Defence in Donnington, Shropshire from where he retired at sixty. During his time at Donnington, Reg regularly received tins of tea from 'his companies' and often spoke about the hard life of the workers on the plantations. After Reg passed away everyone was surprised to find that his shares were worth about half a million pounds. Whether Reg ever realised the value of his investments we shall never know, but it is doubtful if it would have changed the way he lived.

Silverdale Man Arrested for Murder

This story really rocked Silverdale in 1958 when Lucien Gruska was arrested for the murder of the housekeeper of the Roman Catholic priest in London Road, Newcastle. She was returning from visiting friends and entered the front of the house through a large gate on London Road. Gruska must have seen her go in through the gate and in to the garden, where he quickly followed her. He attacked her, then quickly left leaving her lying there. She was found later but sadly she had died.

The following morning at 9am I opened my hairdressing salon to find Mr Gruska my first customer. He seemed perfectly normal and we chatted about different things. My wife, who had just made a pot of tea, brought me a cup in to the salon, Gruska leaned forward in the chair and took my wife's hand pretending to take the tea from her. He held on to my wife's hand for a moment and then passed the tea to me, jokingly asking where his cup was.

My wife returned to our living accommodation and that was the end of that. After having his hair cut he went cheerily on his way. Later that afternoon word went round the village like wildfire that Gruska had been arrested for the housekeeper's murder. My wife, Audrey, was horrified to think that he had held her hand that morning after killing this poor lady. Gruska was a very good worker at the colliery. His friends at work and villagers had been very forgiving to him because he had just served a three year prison sentence for attacking a girl on Silverdale. He got his job back at the colliery because people said he had done his time - let's forgive and forget. Sadly this was how he repaid them. He was given a long sentence, obviously never returning to Silverdale.

Silverdale Lady killed by Stray Shell

Everyone thought at the time that a bomb had been dropped and landed in Newcastle Street Silverdale in 1944. It struck a terraced house, travelled through the roof and unfortunately Eunice Stubbs who was in bed asleep was killed. The mystery was that no sirens had gone off to alert the village of an air raid or approaching enemy aircraft. It was later discovered that it was a stray shell which had been fired at enemy aircraft in a raid over Crewe. The shell had travelled all that way to land on the house.

Anyone who has seen the War Memorial at the front of St. Luke's Church will note that Eunice Stubbs is the only lady's name on the stone. Dr. Johnson of Mill Street who ran his surgery from home was called to the scene. He bravely decided to go in to the badly damaged property and found Eunice, unfortunately already dead in her bed. Dr. Johnson was awarded a wartime commendation for his bravery and his certificate hung proudly on his surgery wall until he retired.

Gordon Birchall - "Mr Silverdale Cricket Club"

A Silverdale lad, whose father owned Silverdale Farm which enveloped the Cricket Club. From a child Gordon has suffered illness with severe lung problems and chest complaints, but he always managed to have a cheerful disposition despite his infirmity. When his father sold his farm to the Borough Council, Gordon moved to a house near Keele with a couple of fields, and built hen houses on the land, producing an egg supply, which he took around the village to sell. He did this for many years, and now he is retired, but with modern drugs he looks and feels very well these days. Gordon has always lived for Silverdale C.C. and has been made a life member, and I believe he has a photograph displayed on the pavilion wall.

Little Bit of Silverdale in Cyprus - Peter "Greenwood"- Jones.

I must admit the first time I heard this name I had not got a clue who it was. But it was Peter Jones of Abbey Sreet Silverdale, who we all knew as Pete. He had added this hyphenated Greenwood. He grew up on Silverdale in Abbey Street, one of three brothers, eldest to Bernard and David. He went to Silverdale Infants and Junior School before passing his 11-plus to Wolstanton Grammar School.

He did a few years in the army, then went into teaching and from there joined the prison service in the education department. His wife Pam was also in the education service at Crewe and Alsager College. They lived in Alsager for a few years and then moved back to Silverdale in High Street.

Peter was a very good crown green bowler and played for Silverdale Conservative Club. One of his loves was singing along with his Dad Fred in the Daleian's Choir. Going on holiday to Cyprus one year he and Pam fell in love with the place, bought a small house and spent as much time as possible out there. They sold this house to buy a piece of land on which they had a new house built. They were both nearing retirement and decided to live in Cyprus, where I believe they have settled down really well. Pam and Peter have both learned to speak the language, and get on with the locals.

A recent visitor to them tells me that Peter has started a choir in the village; could this be the "Daliens Cypriot Section", coming over sometime to Silverdale to give us a concert. Peter obviously decided to keep his Silverdale connections by keeping his Mum and Dad's old house in Abbey Street where one of their sons now lives. So good luck to Pam and Peter, just to let them know they have not been forgotten.

Simpy Sumnall

Over the years Silverdale Colliery had several watchmen. One was Simpy Sumnall. He lived at the top end of the Brighton Cottages and was what was known as a dog man. One particular dog he had was a spotted dalmation and you could see Simpy coming from a long distance because the dog stood out. He was seen as an authority and people would take their dogs along for advice on ailments. A common problem was that the dog would not eat; Simpy would say leave it with me for a day or two. After they had gone he would fasten the dog up in his shed with nothing but a bowl of water and leave it there until it was time to return it to the owner. This worked wonders for the dog and when it returned to its owner its appetite was fully restored. This did Simpy's reputation a power of good in the local community and it often bought him an extra pint or two from many grateful dog owners.

Harry Bonsall

A really lovely, hardworking man, whose first business was as a coal merchant. He eventually sold this and bought premises on the High Street which had been an undertakers. It had a pleasant detached house, a small office and storage space at the bottom of the yard. Harry added to this a petrol pump, the only one at the time on the village. He and his wife Vera ran this very successfully for many years. If Harry was not there, Mrs Bonsall would come out of the house to serve petrol or paraffin. Always with a smile and a friendly quiet word.

Harry worked mainly in the office or down his yard. He always smoked heavily even when serving petrol. When he had filled up he would take his rag to wipe any surplus petrol off the car and put the rag back into the hand which held his cigarette. It was a wonder he never got blown up! At about ten o'clock in the evening he would lock up the pumps and head for the Royal Oak next door. He loved a drink and a game of cards with Ernie Grafton, "Graf" as everyone knew him. Many times the game would be disrupted because someone had run out of petrol and tracked down Harry to the Oak. He would never refuse anyone and he would go and serve them, then back to his card game.

He always wore a flat cap and brown overalls, but in later years he had a boiler suit in dark and light blue checks, very smart! Anyone who remembers him will tell you what a lovely chap he was. I remember when he had his first airline put in, with it being a new thing people were queuing up to use it to check their tyres.

When Mr Ryder sold him his undertaker's business he left a hearse and one day he took this hearse for a ride around the village, apparently it broke down and he left it parked on the pavement. The police must have gone past, seen it, booked it, and Harry was fined £2 in court. Looking around nowadays the police would have a field day, everyone seems to park on the pavement.

Dickie Ward

Lots of people ask me if I remember Dickie Ward in Newcastle Street. He was a very small man who was a real village character. Silverdale always had an excellent Carnival Day once a year and Dickie's contribution was dressing up cycles. He used dozens of sheets of crepe paper of all colours, and would make all sorts of shapes and figures and they won him many prizes in this category. The only thing he ever worried about was if it rained on Carnival Day when all his hard work was quickly ruined. One year he won the best turned out competitor when he dubbed himself black all over and made a grass skirt and went as a Caribbean dancer.

Frank Procter

Frank is a well-known sight on the Dale - never a day passes but that he is seen cycling on his trusty old bike in the village or to Newcastle for his shopping. He was born in Victoria Street in 1917 and played cricket for Silverdale from a young boy through to his forties. He worked for the Coal Board in the Estates and Subsidence division.

Rev. Elliot Booth, St. Luke's Church of England

Rev. and Mrs Booth, with their daughter Jane, arrived to take up the ministry at St. Lukes in November 1966. This was his first parish after working in industry from leaving school, at first in coal mining and then as an industrial photographer, before undertaking his theological training.

Frank Procter

The Vicarage was then situated in High Street at its junction with Sneyd Terrace, the last in the row of villas and right next door to the Sneyd Arms (The Bush). The day of Mr Booth's arrival has always remained in my memory, for he turned up in a three-wheeled car known as a 'Bond'. It didn't entirely look right for a vicar; I learned later that he had quite a collection of these Bond cars. The garden of the vicarage was really overgrown and out of control, but Elliot pulled it back to order, toiling long hours until little by little it began to take shape and in two years was transformed.

Many an evening would find him in the 'Bush' for a couple of pints, chatting with the locals. The people felt he was very much one of them, so approachable and in no way standoffish or aloof. His popularity grew and this brought many people back to the church. Perhaps because of his

Dr Jolly's retirement. His wife Margaret is receiving a bouquet from Mrs Dinah Hollins. Also seen are Dr Brian Hollins, Dr Peter Hollins and, extreme right, Dr Gerald Morgan, together with receptionists and office staff.

St Luke's Church Bring and Buy Sale, with the Mayor and Mayoress, Mr and Mrs Bill Nixon and the vicar and his wife, Mr and Mrs Elliot Booth.

working-class background, many people became quite close to him. You always knew where he was when he was out and about, the distinctive sound of his car engine pop-popping around the village was a cause of affectionate amusement.

Around the late 1970s, a new purpose-built vicarage was erected in Pepper Street and 1973 saw Rev. Booth and his family moving in for the next few years, but at the beginning of 1982 he asked to leave St. Luke's to become Chaplain to Industry at Crewe. His resignation was accepted with great sadness and he left Silverdale at the end of the year. His years at Crewe were greatly enjoyed, but unfortunately in 1988 his health deteriorated and sadly he passed away in 1990.

Seeing Double in Wales

This summer my sister-in-law Mrs Doris Williams, who lives in the bungalows on Farmer's Bank, went on holiday to North Wales with Alice and Charlie Davis formerly of Underwood Road. They went out one day to a local beauty spot, parked the car and went for a stroll. Coming the other way was a gentleman, and getting closer they recognised this man as Mr Elliot Booth a former very popular Vicar of St Luke's Church in Silverdale who had passed away four years ago. Alice said, "Hello Mr Booth", and he stopped to speak to them. He told them that he was Elliot Booth's identical twin. Not many people knew he had one and both parties were pleasantly surprised by this meeting.

Dr Brian Hollins

Born and bred in Scot Hay, Brian remained there until he married when he and his wife Dinah moved into one of the Villas in High Street where their two sons Philip and Richard were born. They moved back to Scot Hay to the family home in 1971 when Brian's parents died.

He was a GP to Silverdale for 29 years starting as a partner to Dr Talbot. When Dr Talbot left, Brian joined Drs Jolly, Childs and Hollins - his brother Peter - and the practice moved into a new purpose-built surgery in Vale Street.

Brian could be quite explosive at times, especially if he thought people were trying it on - like getting sick notes when they weren't ill. Many times he told such patients to b...... off and get back to work. One morning he walked into the surgery to find it packed with people - there was a nasty flu around. He walked to reception and called out, "How many of you have the 'flu?" A good 90% put up their hands to which he replied, "Well I don't want it, nor do the receptionists, so go home to bed for 48 hours and take two paracetamol every 4 hours." This is how we all remember Brian, but if anyone was really poorly his manner was completely different and he gave them first class attention.

Away from medicine Brian had two loves in life, his trains and his cars. He bult his own miniature steam train and as the photograph shows he spent many happy afternoons playing train driver at the Brampton, giving children, and their parents and grandparents, rides.

He was also very much a family man, and both his sons have taken his engineering flair into their careers. Philip works at Rists Rover Division and Richard at the Fordson Tractor Company. Brian and his wife Dinah had lately taken to travelling abroad to see other parts of the world, and their plan was for him to retire at 60 and do this more. Sadly Brian died suddenly at the age of 57, a great shock to the Silverdale community. He will always be remembered as a great character -"sadly gone but certainly not forgotten."

Dr Brian Hollins and passengers at Brampton Park

Last steam train to leave Silverdale station taken by Brian Hollins showing his two sons, Phillip and Richard.

Church Street from Crown Street, again looking towards the church spire which dominates the sky.

Harry White's shop to the right of the Roebuck Pub.

Chapter Six
SHOPS ON SILVERDALE 1940-1950

High Street

Silverdale Co-op	Butchers
Morrals	Sweets and Tobacco
Miss Viggars	Cakes and bread
Deakins	Barber Shop
Bennets	Sweets and tobacco
Morral	Newsagent
Yarwood	Off-licence
Fox	Ladies hairdresser
Woodcocks	Bakery
Rhodes	Fish and chips
Basfords	Butchers
Smith and Morris	Grocery provisions
Harrisons	Oatcakes
Bonsalls flowers	Greengrocers
Hurst	Cycle repairs Paraffin
Swetenhams	Grocery
Daniels	Fish and chips
Davies	Chiropodist
Downings	General stores

Newcastle Street

Freakly	Sweets and tobacco
Barratts	Cycle shop
Jones	Sweets and tobacco
Williams	Grocer & greengrocer
Deakin	Barber shop

Church Street: right hand side

Bonnets	Cleaners
Podmore	Clothes
Garners	Seeds, second hand goods
Mrs Ward	Paraffin and hardware
Jim Macarthy	Fish
Tilsley	Greengrocer
Harrisons	Ladies & mens hairdressing
Cotterrils	Sweets
Hardings	Bike repairs
Whetnalls	Fish and chips
Wilkinsons	Cobblers
Silverdale Post Office	

Church Street: left hand side

Durbur's	Pies and confectionery
Happy Hampton	Butchers
Mrs Evans	Cafe
Barkers	Newsagent
John Lowe	High Class Grocer Cheese Specialist

Dorothy Titley	Ladies Fashions
Walter and Clarence Ward	Paints Hardware
Joe Hough	Newsagent and Printer
Mrs. Salt	Wools and Cotton
Bill Moulineaux	Butcher
Morley's	TV and Radio
Arthur Bloomfield	Paint & Wallpaper
Tom Bower's	Optician
Cottrell's	Taxi
Cornwell's	Chemist
Jack Sanders	Ladies and Men's Outfitters
Bert Sutton	Butcher
Jack Hall	Electrical Goods and Battery Charging
Sam Fernehough	Cooked Meats
Nicholades	Off Licence
Ernie Norcup	Barber
Harry White	General Store
Skerratt's	Off Licence
Saunder's	Butcher
Mitchell's	Sweets Tobacco
Percy Rowley	Grocer
Barratt Brothers	Dentists

Bridge Street Shops

Dean's	Sweets Tobacco
Harrisons	Grocers

Victoria Street Shops

Bailey's	Off Licence
Viggars	Sweets Tobacco
Co-op	Grocery Store

Crown Street Shops

Co-op	Furniture Store
Co-op	Offices for the Area
Plants	Oatcakes
Simcock	Shoe Repairs
Fisher	Electrics
Tom Wright	Butcher
Miss Key	Sweets and Confectionery
Wilkinson's	Fish and Chips
Vallco	Ice Cream Parlour
Clogger Fradley	Shoe Repairs

Chapel Street and Five Road Ends

Johnson's	Sweets Tobacco
Cyril Simcock	Grocery
Edgar 'Cobbler'	Cobbler
Skerratt's	Bottling Plant

To say that Silverdale was very well served is an understatement, with 87 shops, 27 pubs, 3 clubs and 4 off-licence premises, 2 oatcake shops and three full-time small bakeries with freshly made bread and cakes delivered to your front door. For many years it had its own police station in Newcastle Street opposite the Wesleyan chapel which housed a sergeant and two constables. Later in the 1960s there was a redevelopment and a new station was built in the High Street which housed a Sergeant on one side, a constable the other and a station office in the middle. Shortly after the new library was built next to the police station.

Doctors also served it well at that time. Dr Johnson had a bungalow in Mill Street which is now

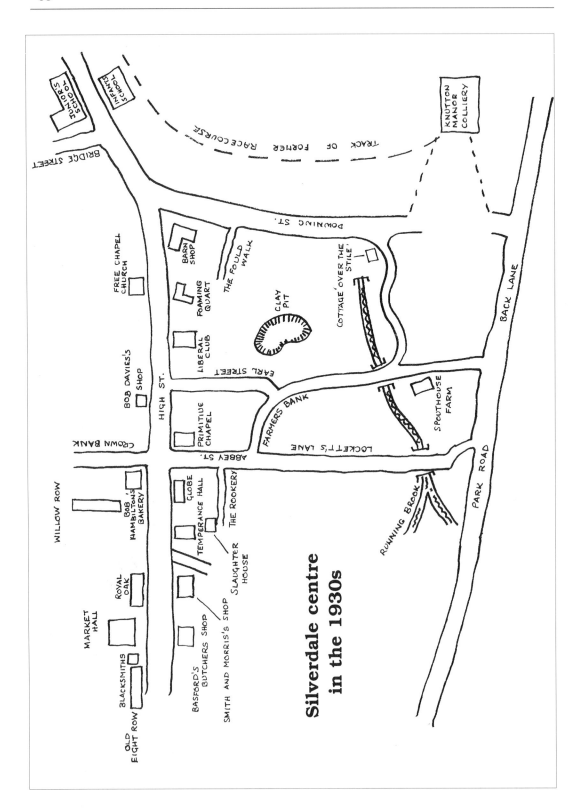

**Silverdale centre
in the 1930s**

a working mens' club. Dr Talbot and Dr Hollins were on the High Street, which is now Warren Brooks bookmakers, and Dr Jolly was in Church Street next to the old post office. All this a far cry from today with the new surgery on Earl Street which houses five doctors, five or six receptionists, nurses, chiropody, acupuncture, physiotherapy and small operations, plus a practice manager who also runs the same practice at the Rycroft Surgery in Newcastle.

My Parents' Shop

We owned a fruit and vegetable shop on the corner of Crown Bank and Newcastle Street which my Mother ran very successfully with the help of two or three assistants, while my father worked at Silverdale Colliery as an overman underground. When he finished his work, he would deliver greengroceries around Knutton, Alsager's Bank and Black Bank with his horse "Dolly" (see photograph). My Father and myself would often arrive home in the dark with two small paraffin lamps for lighting because there were hardly any street lights. I remember him saying that he used to carry a big stick alongside him, in case someone tried to attack him and take his money.

Valcoe's Ice Cream Parlour

Alf arrived from Italy with his wife, four sons and four daughters. He opened his parlour in an old Pub in Crown Bank which retained the seating of the old lounge seats all round the sides, and large wooden tables, with large iron legs. They came from far and wide for Mr Valcoe's ice cream and drinks. And there was always a few local characters who liked to play on his one-armed bandits, discreetly hidden on one side of the saloon.

He made all of his own ice cream and soda drinks on the premises, and he sold lots of ice cream put in to a glass, topped up with your own choice of flavour. He, and his wife and family were lovely people. They were my parents' neighbours for many years. When Mr. Valcoe died, his wife moved into a flat in Underwood Road. She has now passed away, but her family still live around the Silverdale area. When one looks back, it makes you wonder how much ice cream he must have sold to keep his family!

My Hairdressing Career

My hairdressing career started in Church Street, Silverdale, with a five year apprenticeship, to Alf Harrison, who was a very good men's hairdresser. In 1947 he had the foresight to open a ladies salon in a room over the top of the men's salon. About this time Rists factory were taking a lot of ladies in to their factory. This was one of the first time ladies had gone out to work as most had just been housewives and this meant that they had money for the first time to spend on their appearance and having their hair done. This was a wonderful success for Alf Harrison, who took his wife and daughter Sheila in to the business, plus two other hairdressers to cope with the very busy salon.

At this time in the gents' salon most men had a trim every two weeks and most older clients were still being shaved three times a week. We did about thirty shaves on Saturday. Mr. Harrison would often comment that when his grandfather owned the salon in his day he would do 240 shaves on Saturday to earn £1.00, which was one penny per shave. The salon had opened at 8am and closed at 10pm - what a long hard day! A service which was one penny extra was 'singeing', which involved using a long wax taper which was lit and with skilful use of the comb would go all round the hair which had just been trimmed. The theory was that it would stop people catching colds after their trim! The smell was awful, just like burning flesh. One little trick we used to do was to allow the flame to catch some loose hair making it flare which was quite spectacular, especially if any children were watching, they thought it was magic.

Anyone going grey at this time would like us to put some Morgan's pomade on to their hair, a product which would hide grey hair. It worked quite well unless it was stopped when the grey hair would go a horrible yellow colour which took months to fade - or otherwise had to be completely cut out. It looked so comical, normal colour on top with a yellow band round the bottom hairline, so everyone knew what these people were using.

Hairdressing standards had to be kept high because their were three other men's hairdressers on the village - Jack Deakin, Arthur and Louis Deakin and Ern Norcup - so there was no room for complacency. I left Alf in 1955 to work in Stoke for one year but went back to Silverdale in 1956 to open my own salon. Alf Harrison sold his salon and retired to live in Whitchurch near his daughter Sheila.

A Hair-raising Haircut

A five year old boy was taken by his mum to Jack Deakin's in Church Street to have his first proper haircut before going to school. His hair had always been cut at home before. Mum and son took a seat and began to watch the proceedings.

The man in the chair was having a shave with his face all lathered up in soap. Mr Deakin began to shave him, when the man shouted, "Hey, you've cut me." Without more ado, Mr Deakin took a tissue and sure enough there was blood to be seen. It was soon 'cleaned up' and Mr Deakin finished the shave and dried the man's face.

The man sat up in the chair and the haircutting gown was put round him. In those days there were no electric clippers, just hand ones which sometimes got stuck which could be quite painful. Ten minutes later the job was done and the man was off. "Who's next?" said Mr Deakin, putting a plank across the chair arms. "It's Harold next," said Mum, so Harold climbed onto the seat, feeling terrified by this time, after what he had just seen.

On went the gown. "Just keep still and it won't hurt you," said Mr Deakin, placing his left hand in a vice like grip on top of Harold's head. Harold began to cry and tried to wriggle and the clippers soon got stuck. "Keep your head still," was all he could hear. The clippers were freed and the job was eventually completed.

"There, that wasn't so bad," said Mr Deakin. He reached across to his water spray to put some on Harold's hair. He aimed the spray but the cold water went straight across the back of Harold's neck. In a flash the terrified youngster leapt out of the chair, out through the door, and never stopped until he reached the 'jitty hole' where he lived.

His mother followed him home to find him vowing never to go back there again. She suddenly realised she had never even paid. When she got back to Jack Deakin's, the other customers were still laughing over Harold's rapid departure and Mr Deakin refused to accept any money - it was the first time anyone had run out on him and he had also had a good laugh. And this little Harold? It was Harold Deville of Cherry Tree Lane who is now 70 and he remembers that haircut as if it was yesterday.

Who Remembers the Dart Cash Carrier?

The Silverdale Co-op Grocery Department in Victoria Street was a very busy shop. There were no tills to pay at - the system was a series of overhead wires leading to an office where the girls waited for the "Dart Cash Carrier" to bring the money to them. The shop assistant would put the bill and the money in to a brass cup, screw the bottom on, pull a lever and this shot the brass cup up on one of the wires to the office. Here the girls would put the change in to the brass cup and return it to the assistant.

It was intriguing to watch a series of these cups flying round the ceiling. One presumes this is where the name came from, darting here and darting there. Apparently these cups were very heavy and all the staff were warned to be careful to fasten them on properly because of the risk of one flying off and landing on someone's head. Being made of brass they would have given a nasty headache.

Jack Sandelance, Greengrocer Church Street

Everyone to this day seems to remember Jack. He was about 5' 6" tall, but weighing around 22 stones was a very portly gentleman. He would help anyone out if he could. He ran a very busy shop with his wife, Doris, who is still living in Silverdale, now aged 90.

Jack Sandelance - everyone you speak to in Silverdale remembers Jack.

He employed Stuart Glover, who lived on the village, and when he was old enough Stuart learned to drive. Jack bought a flat-backed lorry and he used to buy his own produce and collect it instead of having it delivered. He also began to do a little wholesaleing himself and would often help my parents out with produce if they needed anything in our shop which was just down the road from Jack's shop.

On the occasional race day Jack and Stuart would take a group of men off the village to a race meeting and they would leave - and arrive back home, after consuming a few pints - just sitting on the back of the open lorry. Jack had to sit sideways in his seat because he could not close the door properly owing to his size.

Sadly, Jack died suddenly from a heart attack, ending a very colourful life, leaving his widow Doris to run the business. After a while Doris decided to sell the shop and sold out to "Lathams" of Porthill, who still run the business but in the new development on The Parade following the village redevelopment shortly after they took over Jack's shop.

Stuart Glover went on to work for Eddie Tilsley and stayed with him for many years. He still works today on Newcastle market selling fruit and vegetables, standing out in all weathers. I have never known Stuart to be ill!

Cobbler Fradley

Mr Fradley was a small man with a mop of black hair and dark thick-rimmed glasses who had a very busy shoe repairers on Crown Street. He had what was known as a club foot where he had one shoe built up about four inches giving a massively thick sole which made it very heavy. When he walked, he virtually dragged his foot behind him. When he was working at his shoes he sat in the window of his shop almost sitting on the pavement, and always with a mouthful of nails perhaps thirty at a time. The local children would creep up to the window and start pulling faces at him. This really upset him and he would hobble out of the shop waving his walking stick, but by this time the kids were long gone. He would go to shout at the kids and all his nails would fall from his mouth. Back he would waddle to his stool, reload with nails and hammer away on his shoe last.

Fisher Electrics, Crown Street

Fred Fisher opened his shop selling television and radio sets and also did outside contract work. His son Boyce worked in the shop learning the trade with his Dad. At this time TVs were all black and white with seven inch screens, and when the lights in the room had to be turned off to see the picture.

Bowler dies in tragic repeat

A BOWLER has collapsed and died on the green in a tragic repeat of his father's death.

Mr Boyce Fisher, 53, suffered a heart attack in his debut for Burslem Suburban against Meir Kings Arms in the North Stafford-shire Amateur League.

His father Fred also died during a game against the Meir team while playing for Silverdale Conserva-tives 10 years ago.

The latest tragedy happened on Suburban's green at High Lane.

By Andy Walpole

Mr Fisher, father of two, of High Street, Silverdale, joined the club from Silverdale Conservatives, where he had been a member for about 15 years, this season.

The match — Suburban's first of the season — was called off after the tragedy.

Bowlers tried to revive Mr Fisher by wrapping him in blankets and giving him heart massage. He died moments before the ambulance arrived.

Mr Fisher, who had a history of heart trouble, had represented the Potteries and District County team.

Before taking early retirement, he worked at Hem Heath Colliery. He leaves a widow and two sons.

County bowls team manager Graham McGarry said of Mr Fisher: "He was a very good character, and well liked."

After a couple of years Boyce decided he did not like the work so he left and went to work as an apprentice at Silverdale Colliery. Mr Fisher could not cope with both the shop and the contracting on his own so he closed the shop to concentrate on the contracting side.

Fred's main love outside his work was his bowling. He played for Silverdale Conservative Club and became a county bowler for many years. Boyce followed in his footsteps but sadly collapsed and died playing bowls at Burslem Suburban Club.

Roger, Boyce's brother had joined his father in the business. Fred has now passed away but Roger has carried the business on to this day. His son Roger in turn has carried on the family sporting tradition by becoming a professional golfer and is currently trying to make his way on the golf circuit.

John Roberts and Son

John Roberts opened his own business in Silverdale in a very small garage in Cross Street. He then added a second garage at the Rookery in Silverdale, which he bought from Mrs Hampton. A lot of hard work was done in these garages, working seven days per week up to eighteen hours per day. His son Anthony joined him when he left school and worked alongside his Dad learning the trade.

The story goes that Mr Roberts was in Harry Bunsall's yard one day and spotted an old 1924 Armstrong-Siddely. Asking Harry how much he wanted for this motor, Harry said forty quid. Mr Roberts went home to his wife to get the money, telling her what a bargain he had got. But when Mrs. Roberts saw the bargain she was not amused - it looked a wreck to her. But John persuaded her. He and Anthony set about restoring the car and it is now in beautiful condition and Anthony drives it every year in the London to Brighton Rally and also uses it for the odd wedding. Mrs Roberts must feel very proud when she looks at the car now.

Getting back to the garages, they were getting very busy and their premises were not really big enough to cope with their workload. Then the first business park was being built at Stonewall Estate and Newcastle Borough Council were encouraging them to move to these new premises. They closed down both garages and moved to a large unit in 1966 and through sheer hard work have expanded now into transport, cranes and diesel vehicle specialists. John Roberts has passed away now leaving Anthony to run the business which has now gone from strength to strength with hard work and attention to detail.

Morley's Radio and Television

This store from the Ironmarket Newcastle, decided to expand into a second shop in Church Street Silverdale. They opened a large shop with a repair workshop at the rear of the premises and an excellent display of television sets and radios. The manager was a chap named Don Till who became very popular with Silverdale people. He was also an excellent engineer. The other engineers were Bill

Brighton Cottages with the pit mound in the background.
Brighton Cottages were very close to the railway crossing which entered the colliery grounds. When they were demolished a new nursing home was built on the site, named Brighton House.

Fred Fisher loved his hobby - playing the violin.

Roger Fisher, grandson of Fred, is now
a professional golfer.

Rookery Garage was owned and operated by John Roberts and his son Anthony.

Mr Roberts with his 1925 Armstrong Siddeley

Victoria Street. The large double-fronted shop housed the main grocery store - this was the shop which used the Dart Cash Carrier.

Lowe's grocery shop in Church Street.

1950s, with Dorothy Titley and assistant in her Church Street shop.

At the rear of Woodcock's Bakery with Paddy the horse, held by Mr Woodcock. Daughter Lily, then aged six, stands alongside. Lily is now Mrs Ted Trotter and has just celebrated her 90th birthday. She lives with her daughter Lilian and son-in-law Dave.

Woodcock's Bakery and Confectioners, High Street 1930, showing Bob and his sister Lily in the doorway.

Bradely and Don Till's two nephews Ken and Brian Ross who were identical twins. This was a very successful business for the Morley family.

At this time myself and the Ross twins were trying to start a football team in the Thursday half holiday league, but all being apprentices at the time we could not afford the league fees. The Morley family were approached and they agreed to buy us a full strip of shirts, shorts and socks and the team was named Morley's Radio and TV Football Club. Our first season was a disaster, played eighteen games, lost seventeen, drew one. But after the first season and a couple of new players, we did quite well for a few years even reaching the semi-final of the Haig & Haig trophy which was the half holiday league cup.

In the meantime Don Till decided to open his own shop just across the road which took a lot of Morley's business away and the Morley family eventually decided to close the business. The Ross twins Brian and Ken decided to carry on the shop in their own right and being able to do all their own repairs and servicing did very well. Don Till too was doing very well and needed bigger premises so he moved on to the High Street where he employed Allan Scott a local boy.

Don offered a service of putting TV aerials up. He offered me the chance of earning extra pocket money by paying me one pound per aerial fixed. I drove the van and Allan Scott provided the technical know-how. We both earned good money at this especially on Sundays.

The Ross twins were caught up in the redevelopment of Church Street and they moved to a new shop in the Parade. They continued to trade from there for years but due to mounting opposition from the large multiples they decided to move to a town shop in Burslem where they still are now.

Bakeries

There were several bakeries where bread and cakes made fresh each day and delivered by bicycle or on foot with large baskets. **Bird's Bakery** in Ford Street were renowned for their vanilla slices. Children would queue there for bags of bits at the end of the day. A large bag would only cost one penny old money. **Braddock's Baker** was lovely bread especially their large cobs which were always sold out by lunch time. It was hard work and long hours but excellent job satisfaction. **Woodcock's Shop and Bakery** on the High Street The shop sold confectionery and bread. Bob made lovely ice buns which were very popular with the American troops stationed at Keele. Ken Billington told me about when the Americans were assembling to leave the area. They were all crowded onto Silverdale Station and they were giving Ken and his mates two bob each to fetch these buns from Woodcock's Bakery to eat on their journey home. Sorry - two bob in old money was two shillings, in present currency ten pence. Ken reckoned they made pounds that day when £3-4 would be a week's wages, besides the presents of chewing gum and sweets. The village boys were very sorry to see the Americans leave.

Jim McCarthy

Well known as "Fish Jim" he sold fruit, vegetables, cigarettes, sweets, chocolate and wet fish. What a combination. With no fridges or freezers at that time anyone walking past Jim's shop would have been in no doubt that he sold fish. He bought his fish on Monday and would still be selling the same fish on Saturday. No wonder there was the odd tummy bug among Jim's customers on Silverdale.

Jim was a bachelor and lived many years in lodgings in Sneyd Terrace. His shop was his life, and his pastime was playing cards every evening in Silverdale Conservative Club with his friends. I remember him telling us the story of the Inland Revenue called him in to the tax office for an explanation as to why he had not sent any tax returns in for five years. He pleaded total ignorance and said that he had not made any profit for five years. The tax people began an inquiry into Jim's affairs. Looking into his financial situation, they realised that he was not trying to fiddle his books, he just did not know what to do with accounts. They sent inspectors who realised that he could not be doing much business with the chaos of the place and the "fishy smell" of the premises. The Inland Revenue informed him that he would not be prosecuted provided he produced annual accounts from then on. Jim was a one-off Irish character who came to Silverdale in the 1940s and stayed until his death in the1960s.

Butcher Basford's Slaughterhouse
On Mondays the Silverdale butchers would go to Market Drayton market and buy their own beast to last them all the week. The cattle would come by train in cattle trucks to Silverdale Station. They would then be driven to their various premises. These animals would be slaughtered at the rear of the shops. Besides the sale of meat all the butchers processed the offal obtained from the beast. There would be bacon, sausage, brawn, tongue, ham and savory ducks. Before balloons became popular lads would run round the village with pig's bladder tied to the end of a stick.

The Cooperative
The Co-op used horse drawn vans and traps to do all their deliveries. Mr. Ball actually made these vans and their wheels on his premises, Mr. Fenton was the blacksmith who also looked after all the horses shoes and this was a perfect combination. In winter time these horses and traps would be seen queuing to have specially sharpened studs fitted to their shoes, when it was icy or snowing. The stable door was open at the top half and closed at the bottom. You could see the sparks flying everywhere inside. The hammers striking the anvil made a lovely ringing sound, which would change with the heavy hammer to flatten and shape the red hot metal. Suddenly you could not see for steam as Mr Fenton plunged the red hot metal in to a large steel drum of cold water to cool down the shoes and studs before fitting them to the horses.

Emlyn's Nursery
This was run from a small terraced house in Abbey Street where Mrs Emlyn was well known for her skills in buttonholes and bouquets for weddings, and wreaths, crosses, etc for funerals. I believe at one time there was a kind of exotic plant in their greenhouse called Oukernotia and the only other one in the country was in Kew Gardens in London.

Coal Merchants on Silverdale
In the1940s and early fifties coal merchants delivered on a daily basis all round the village. It was very hard work, dirty, heavy, carrying one hundredweight (1 cwt = 50 Kg) wet sacks up steps and down entries. They wore a heavy leather protector for their backs and shoulders to try and keep them dry. But on wet winter's days this did not offer much protection when the wet sacks had turned to ice. They would get home filthy dirty and wet through every day and had to take a hot bath to ease their aching limbs.

Landy Williams ran his business from his home in Newcastle Street where the large double gates still stand. He kept his lorry and coal in the yard at the rear of the premises. This business is still run today by Norman Ellis from The Villas in High Street. He married Mabel Johnson the granddaughter of Mr Williams.

Albert and Jim Lee ran another busy coal merchants withtwo or three lorries. Albert lived in Mill Street and he employed two or three lads besides Doug Lowndes of Newcastle Street. Doug took over the business after Albert retired and carried on for many years until he retired.

The Co-op also ran a couple of lorries around the village with Albert Ward, Joe Hadgett, Harry Boulton and Ernest Buckley doing the deliveries.

Ben Clegg of Farmers bank employed Bernard Walker to deliver his coal and Reg Burgess of

May Street was self-employed and remained a one-man band.

Silverdale Miners Union delivered their own miner's coal with Frank O'Leary, Fred Sumnal and Ken Fernihough providing a very good service. Peter Lomax still delivers coal around the village as he has done for many years.

I think it is easy to see what a pall of smoke hung over the village in those days with all the houses burning coal let alone the industries.

Reg Lee, Forge Garage - halfway between Silverdale and Newcastle

As a young man Reg Lee lived in the first house in Mill Street, backing onto the racecourse fields, where he spent many hours on his motor bikes racing round the fields practising and improving his technique. Eventually he set his mind on doing the Isle of Man T.T.

He moved from Mill Street and bought the house next door to my parents so we got to know Reg very well. He was a lovely character who certainly knew no fear when he got astride a motor bike. When he eventually got in to the Isle of Man T.T. he had his new bike delivered to the garage ready for tuning. On Sunday morning nice and early he would ride down to Pooldam and race back to Stonewall for test runs. Needless to say the noise woke everyone up and people were turning out to watch him flying by.

He did the T.T. for several years but in his last year he had a brilliant ride and was leading wih only a short distance to go when he went over a humpback bridge where just previously another rider had come off. The officials had managed to get the bike and rider out of the way but had left a patch of oil on the road. Reg came hurtling over the bridge, touched the oil and came off, injuring himself quite badly.

He and his wife decided it was time for him to retire from this very dangerous sport. He moved and bought the end house right by the garage and settled down to running the garage. He has since retired and his son David, who now in turn employs his son Chris, runs the garage. They do M.O.T. testing and David rents the parts off to different mechanics and a body repair shop.

Petrol Stations

There were two petrol stations on the village. One was at the Swan Pub in Mill Street, which was run by Paddy Darcy and his wife. There was one hand pump for petrol and another for paraffin.

As cars became more popular more petrol was needed on the village so Harry Bonsall opened a station on the High Street next door to the Royal Oak Pub. This was "open all hours", seven days a week, eighteen hours a day. Besides petrol and paraffin he sold secondhand goods and was always one for a bargain.

Taxis

Even in the 1930-1940 era Silverdale had a taxi service run by Cottrells, next door to Cornwells Chemist. Goodness knows who used a taxi in those times - enough though to make a living for the Cottrell family.

BUY YOUR

AT

MRS. BARKER'S,

MANCHESTER HOUSE,

CHURCH-STREET, SILVERDALE.

Kellys Directory for Silverdale in the mid-1930s

SILVERDALE is a large village and civil parish, and with part of Knutton and Scothay, was formed Dec. 14, 1855, into an ecclesiastical parish from the civil parishes of Audley, Keele and Silverdale, and into a civil parish in 1895, by the "Local Government Act, 1894." Silverdale is governed by the Wolstanton United Urban District Council, formed in 1904. There is a station here on a branch of the North Stafford railway from Stoke to Market Drayton, and the village is 2 miles west from Newcastle-under-Lyme, included with Newcastle-under-Lyme for parliamentary purposes, in the hundred and petty sessional division of Pirehill North, county court district of Newcastle-under-Lyme, union of Wolstanton and Burslem, rural deanery of Newcastle-under-Lyme, archdeaconry of Stoke-upon-Trent and diocese of Lichfield. The church of St. Luke, consecrated October 28th, 1853, is an edifice of stone in the Gothic style, consisting of chancel, nave, aisles, south porch and a tower at the east end, with spire, containing a clock and 8 bells, provided by public subscription at a cost of £500, and hung in 1907: the church was restored in 1888, at a cost of £600, and affords about 520 sittings. The register dates from the year 1853. The living is a vicarage, net yearly value £303, with residence, in the gift of Ralph Sneyd esq. D.L., J.P. and held since Dec. 1914, by the Rev. Selwyn Leighton Buckwell, Lichfield Th. College. The Mission church of St. Paul at Scothay is an edifice of brick, consisting of apsidal chancel, nave, west porch and a turret containing one bell, and will seat 100 persons. The hamlet it supplies consists of about 300 inhabitants, and lies a mile N.W. from the parish church. The Mission church of St. Andrew, in High street, is a building of corrugated iron on brick foundations, consisting of nave, apsidal chancel, vestries and a turret with spire: it was purchased from the vicar of All Saints, Weston-super-Mare, Somerset, rebuilt at a cost of £800, and dedicated by the Bishop of Shrewsbury April 13, 1904: it will seat about 350 persons. The Catholic church of the Sacred Heart, in Victoria street, formerly used as a school, is served from Newcastle. There are also Congregational, Wesleyan Methodist, Primitive Methodist and United Methodist chapels and Salvation Army hall. A Primitive Methodist chapel was erected at Cross Heath in 1911. A cemetery of 3 acres was formed in 1886, at cost of £1,200; it has a mortuary chapel of iron, and i under the control of the Parish Council. The Conserva tive Club, in Church street, was erected in 1876 at th expense of the late Rev. Walter Sneyd, and comprise reading, billiard, dining and refreshment rooms. Her are extensive iron and coal works. Ralph Sneyd esc D.L., J.P. who is lord of the manor, and the repre sentatives of the late Luke Bennett esq. are the prin cipal landowners. The extent of the parish is 1,82 acres, inclusive of 4 of water; rateable value, £29,075 the population in 1911 was 7,795; the population o the ecclesiastical parish (St. Luke) was 6,126 and th acreage is 830.

Post, M. O., T. & T. E. D. Office.—John France, sub postmaster. Letters arrive through Newcastle-under Lyme

Wall Letter Box, Cross Heath

County Police, Cross Heath, John Walker, constable

Police Station, George Nadin, inspector, 1 sergeant ̷ 5 constables

The fire appliances, the property of the Wolstantor United Urban District Council, are kept in th Council yard, High street

Public Elementary Schools.

The schools are under the control of the Wolstantor United Urban District Education Committee

Director, William Willis, Moreton house, Wolstanton

Secretary, Edward Hollinshead, Moreton ho. Wolstantor

Council, erected in 1877 & infants' in 1886, for 320 boys 380 girls & 216 infants; Frank Ellams, master; Mis Annie Cook, girls' mistress; Miss Mercy Drury infants' mistress

Church of England, built in 1831, at the expense of the late Ralph Sneyd esq. & enlarged in 1894, for 18c boys, 176 girls & 131 infants; Caleb John Yates master; Miss Gertrude Johnson, n istress; Mis E. Mortiboy, infants' mistress

Cross Heath (mixed), built in 1876, for 100 children; Miss Amelia James, mistress

North Staffordshire Railway Station, John Peake, sta tion master & goods agent

PRIVATE RESIDENTS.

(For T N's see general list of Private Residents at end of book.)

Alsop Frederick J. Parkfields

Cocks John, Silverdale house

Daly Louis Alfred L.M.S.S.A. Louis villa, High st

Davies John Owen, The Villas, High street

Doherty Rev. P. (Roman Catholic), The Presbytery, Downing st

Ellams Frank, Sneyd villas, High st

Glover Rev. Wm. (Primitive Methodist), Maycroft, High st

Goodwin Capt. Fleming Gradwell, Red heath

Heath Rev. Stephen Francis L.Th. (curate), The Vicarage

Howlett Rev. Edwin John Evans M.A. (vicar), The Vicarage

Johnson Miss G. A. The Villas, High street

Johnson Percy George M.B., Ch.B. The Bungalow, Mill street

Morris George, Sneyd villas, High st

Morris John Sydney, Park road

Small Everard, The Villas, High st

COMMERCIAL.

Early closing day, Thursday.

Marked thus ° farm 150 acres or over.

Abberley Ernest, insur. agt. 152 Church st

Allchurch Benj. beer retlr. 86 Church street

Allman Herbert, pork butcher, 13 Church street

Allsopp Chas. grocer, 92 Church st

Ashton Wm. plumber, 83 Church st

Baggaley Letty (Mrs.),fried fish dlr. 123 Church st

Barker Arth.P. stationer,24 Church st

Barratt Samuel Harold, dentist, 106 Church street

Barratt Thomas Edward, dentist, 118 Church street

Barratt Wm. cycle dlr. 104 New-Castle st

Basford Wm. butcher, 81 High st

Beech Caleb, grocer, 1 Vale st

Beeston Mary Alice (Mrs.), beer retlr. 53 High st

Bird Jn. baker, 78 Church st

Bonnett Jn. Edwd. fried fish dlr. 9 Church st. & motor bus propr. see Garbett & Bonnett

Bonsall Bros. nurserymen, Park rd

Bonsall Jsph. Hy. bldr. 62 High st

Booth Harry, shopkpr. 16 Book st

Bostock Edna (Miss), confctnr. 14 Chapel st

Bowers W. & Son, watch makers, 48 Church street

Bowler Agnes (Miss), confctnr. 60 High st

Brown Ethel (Mrs.), shopkpr. 16 Bridge st

Brown Fred, shoe maker, 61 & 63 High street

Brown Jas. beer retlr. Five Ways end, Vale Pleasant

Burdon Lavinia (Mrs.), Swan inn, 3 Mill st. T N 18

Burgess Caleb, shopkpr. 79 Victoria st

Burgess Geo. coal mer. 6 Kinsey st

Caple William Morrison, insurance supt. Gordon house, High street

Cartlidge Jsph. greengro. 121 Newcastle st

Chattin Harriett (Miss), draper, 36 Church st

Clegg Jas. Chas. smallholder, Spout House farm

Cooper Marjory (Miss), ladies' hairdrssr. 1 George st

Cornwell T. C. chemist & druggist, 52 & 54 Church st. T N 3

Cottrell Arth. Royal Oak hotel, High st

Cotterill Peter, confctnr. 50 Church st. T N 26

Cumberbatch Wm. greengro. 76 Church st

Dale Wm. insur. agt. 125 Church st

Daly Louis Alfd. L.M.S.S.A.Lond. school medical inspector & police surgn. for Silverdale, Keele & Knutton, Louis villa, High st. & 113 Church st. T N 11

Davies Annie (Mrs.), midwife, 51 Vale Pleasant

Deacon Clara (Mrs.), confctnr. 17 Church st

Deakin Arth. hairdrssr. 126 High st

Deakin Jn. Thos. hairdrssr. 7 Church st

Dean Fred, shopkeeper, 3 Bridge st

District Bank Limited (sub-branch) (Herbert Lee, manager) (open on

District Bank Limited (sub-branch) (Herbert Lee, manager) (open on tues. & fri. from 11 a.m. to 1 p.m.), 122 Church street; head office, Spring gardens, Manchester

Dix Ann (Mrs.), Crown inn, Crown st

Downing Geo. Kinsey, bldr. Vale st. T N 52

Downing Nellie (Miss), grocer, 3 High st

Drill Hall (Danl. Jones, propr.), Park rd

°Durber Harry, farmer, Sneyd villas, High st

East End Working Men's Club (Arth. Tunnicliffe, sec.), 11 Newcastle st

Edwards Lucy (Mrs.), shopkpr. 34 Chapel st

Edwards Saml. Wm. plumber, 109 High st

Ellams Martha (Mrs.), milliner, 22 Church st

Embling Thos. florist, Abbey st

Fenton Wm. Thos. smith, High st

Fernyhough Saml. butcher, 6a Church st

Finnemore Jn. Wm.shopkpr.Abbey st

Forrester Albt. Joshua, butcher, 55 High st

Forrester Geo. butcher, 63 Church st

Fradley Arth. boot repr. 1 & 2 Crown st

Freakley Jas. shopkpr. 3 Newcastle st

Garbett & Bonnett,motor bus proprs. Church st

Glover Alfd. billiard hall propr. 30 High st

Green Albt. Jn. blacksmith, Abbey st

Green James, confectnr. 125 High st

Hall Jn. tobccnst. 60 Church st

Hampton Wm. butcher, 14 Church st. T N 46

Harding Edith Y. (Miss), tobccnst. 40 Church st

Harrison Alfd. hairdrssr.57 Church st

Harrison Jsph. Thos. shopkpr. 4 & 5 Bridge st

Hazlehurst Jn. clerk & registrar to Silverdale Cemetery, Cemetery la

Hewitt Harriet (Miss), confctnr. 12 Church st

Holden Ellen M. (Mrs.), cycle dlr. 85 Church st

Hough Jas. Fredk.statnr.38Church st

Jackson Jsph. fried fish dlr. 37 High st

Johnson Percy Geo. M.B., Ch.B. physcn. & surgn. The Bungalow, Mill st. T N 49

Jones Hilda Ann (Mrs.), confctnr. 101 Newcastle st

Jones Wm.insur. agt.69 Newcastle st

Keay Wm. Edwd. shopkpr. 39 Vale Pleasant

Lee Charles Hy. shopkpr. 77 High st

Lee Jn. boot repr. 28 Crown st

Lee Saml. draper, 50 Victoria st

Lewis Thomas H. beer retlr. 44 Church st

Lowe Albert, shopkpr. 20 Church st

Lowe John, grocer, 26 Church street

Lowe Wm. Sneyd Arms P.H.High st

Lowndes Frank,confctnr.18Church st

Mellor Rhoda (Miss), shopkpr. 27 Church st

Ministry of Labour Employment Exchange, Wesleyan church, Newcastle st. T N 44

Minshull Mary E. (Mrs.), hardware dlr. 63 Church st

Morrall Geo.Thos. statnr. 128 High st

Morris George, grocer, see Smith & Morris

Morris Jas. Alfd. N. butcher, 45 Church st

Moulton Emily (Mrs.) C.M.B. midwife, 73 Church st

Moulton Mary (Miss), draper, 73 Church st

Mountford Chas. beer retlr. 1 Cemetery la

Mullineux Jsph.butcher,58 Church st

Mullineux Jsph. S. butcher, 42 Church st. T N 1

Norcup Saml. E. hairdrssr. 109 Church st

North Staffordshire Permanent Economic Benefit Building Society (Frank Seabridge, agt.), 71 Newcastle st

Oldbury Jas. fried fish dlr. 28 Chapel st

Osborne Rd. beer retlr. 103 High st

Pearl Assurance Co. Ltd. (Wm. M. Caple, supt.), Gordon ho. High st

Pepper Clara (Mrs.), grocer, 7 Crown st

Phillips Bros. bldrs. May st. T N 63

Platt Edwin, Vine inn, 130 High st

Plim Eleanor E. (Mrs.), butcher, 8 Crown st

Podmore Sarah (Mrs.), draper, 15 Church st

Pover Joseph, tailor, 130 Church st

Queen's Palace Cinema (Wltr.Mason, propr.), High st

Rhodes Thos.fried fish dlr.79 High st

Rogers Saml. shopkpr. 35 High st

Ryder Dudley, bldr. 106a, High st

Ryles Jn. Sidney, beer retlr. 129 Church st

Sandelance Fred, greengro. 46 Church st

Sandelance Mary E. (Mrs.), beer retlr. 66 Church st

Sandelance Sarah (Miss), shopkpr 67 Albert st

Saunders Geo. H. butcher, 94 Church st

Seabridge Frank, carpenter & joiner, 71 Newcastle street

Shelton Iron, Steel & Coal Co. Ltd. colliery proprs. T N 22

Shorthouse Regnld. beer retlr. 95 Newcastle st

Silverdale Aerated Water Co. Ltd. mineral water mfrs. Chapel st. T N 34

Silverdale Cemetery (Jn. Hazelhurst, clerk & registrar), Cemetery lane

Silverdale Conservative Association & Club (Geo. Ellams, hon. sec.), 154 Church st

Silverdale & District Working Men's Club (Hy. Johnson, sec.), 29 Chapel st

Silverdale Equitable Industrial Cooperative Society Ltd. (Edwd. J. Dryhurst, president; Nelson Gartside, sec. & mngr.), Crown st.; Victoria st. (T N 6); Kinsey st. & 30 Church st

Silverdale Tileries Co. brick & tile makers, roofing & ridge tile manufacturers, facings, pavings & channel bricks; works, Silverdale Tileries. T A " Silverdale Tileries, Silverdale, Staffs;" T N Silverdale, 10

Simcock Dan, grocer, 45 High st

Simcock Ellen (Mrs.), hosier, 51 Victoria st

Simcock William, sanitary inspector to Newcastle-under-Lyme Corporation, 25 Abbey st

Simpson Geo. beer retlr. 81 Victoria st

Skerratt Leonard, wine & spirit merchant, 90 Church st. T N 19

Smith & Morris, grocers, 65 High st. T N 23

Sutton Alfd. C. shopkpr. 18 Crown st

Swettenham's Ltd. grocers, 41 & 43 High street

Timmis Alice (Mrs.), grocer, 102 Church st

Tomlinson Annice (Mrs.), confctnr. High st

Townsend Jn. poultry farmer, Red Heath

Valco Goffredo, shopkpr. 3 Crown st

Vickers Nellie (Miss), shopkpr. 148 High st

Viggars John, shopkeepr. 178 High st

Walley Thomas Edward, roofing & ridge tile manufacturers; Rosemary Hill tileries. T A " Roofing, Silverdale;" T N 9

Ward Alfd. hardware dlr. 11 & 33 Church st

Ward Arth. Jn. plumber, 108 High st

Watson J. & Son (Silverdale) Ltd. pawnbrkrs. Albert st

White Harry, shopkpr. 88 Church st

Whittaker Mina (Miss), shopkpr.39a, High st

Wilkinson Thos. boot repr. 107 Church st

Wilkinson Wm. fried fish dlr. 6 Crown st

Williams Thos. Olando, coal dlr. 85 Newcastle st

Winkle F. E. registrar of births, deaths & marriages (mon. 1 to 2 p.m.), Wesleyan church, Newcastle st

Woodcock Frank,beer ret.34Church st

Woodcock Isabella (Mrs.), baker, 83 High st

Wright Thos. butcher, 101 Church st

Yearsley Lilian (Mrs.), confctnr. 98 Newcastle st

Lower part of Church Street looking down towards Newcastle Street. The Foundry chimneys are just visible in the distance.

William Ashton, plumber, glazier, painter and decorator, Church Street.

Below: T.W. Carryer, Pawnbroker, Albert Street.

Reg Lee of Forge Garage on a Norton Junior, 1934 Manx Grand Prix, Isle of Man

Forge Garage c1947. when petrol rationing was still in force.

Harry's petrol pump
Harry Bonsall with his pal
Jack Jepson. Jack owned his
own transport firm and kept
his vehicles in Harry's yard.

Below: There was still petrol
rationing in the 1950s

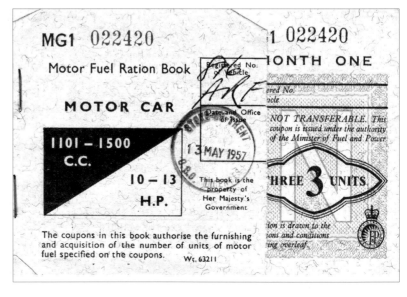

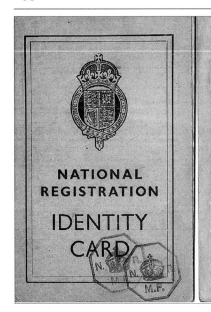

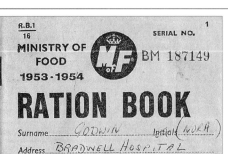

Sister Nora
Godwin's ration
book and Wartime
identity card.

Many people on Silverdale will
remember Sister Godwin (on
left) who was sister at Bradwell
Isolation Hospital for Infectious
Diseases (later TB hospital for
men) during the 1940s.

The Parade
Shopping Precinct
built in the 1960s

Corner of Crown Bank and High Street, showing Elim Church. The shop on the corner was Bonsall's greengrocery in the 1950s. The new Elim Church is currently heading for its third extension - a sign of its popularity. The church is full most Sunday mornings and evenings.

Smith and Morris - Wholesale grocers, High Street

Victoria Street

High Street looking down from the old Belstaff factory on far left to top end of village.

Church Street shops

Church Street - the shopping area.

Jack Morall's newsagent's shop, opposite the Vine Inn on High Street.

Church Street shops. A very busy shopping centre - nearly every property was a shop.

Church Street showing Podmore's old shop, extreme left, Jack Deakin's Barber's Shop (centre) and the Wesleyan Chapel just behind the bus shelter.

Cut price store which took over Swetenham's former High Street premises.

The old Primitive Methodist Chapel High Street.

The Wesleyan Chapel Newcastle Street demolished 1960s.

Chapter Seven
CHURCHES

Methodism on Silverdale

Silverdale has always been known as a Methodist Village. In the 1930-1950 era there were four very strong Chapels, with excellent congregations and that strong competitive feeling between them - like who could produce the best charity show held once a year with children singing on the stage, afternoon and evening. In the morning session the children would assemble at their own Chapel and proceed, led by a brass band, around the street and sing and collect money from the houses. Everyone used to turn out to watch these processions and with all the streets being terraced houses there would be hundreds of people watching.

Every child would have a new outfit for the occasion. Mrs Podmore and Jack Sanders, the very popular clothing and shoe shops, looked forward to these four Sunday anniversaries because all the clothes were bought from these two shops.

After each Chapel's day, at the evening service they would announce the total raised from the two services and street collection and this provided another competition between the Chapels to see who could raise most money.

One comical and memorable little story about the Wesleyan Chapel, of which I was a member, was when we were about to start to sing in Brook Street and Mr Ford, the local milkman, arrived in the street with his horse and milk float. When the drummer of the brass band struck his drum to start us singing, the horse reared up in the air tipping milk churns out on to the road. What a mess! Mr Ford was not very pleased. It was a new horse he was training and the drum had startled it badly. He swore a few times, seeing hundreds of gallons of milk going down the grids. Mr Joe Bailey, Sunday School Superintendent called for Mr Ford to stop swearing and said to him, "Mr Ford, it is Sunday you know, please do not swear in front of these children." I can not remember his answer but he was not a happy man; he would have to wait for hours for more milk to arrive.

Wesleyan Chapel, Newcastle Street

This was a thriving chapel with an excellent congregation and Sunday School. The Redfern family and the Baileys were the main stalwarts. Mathew put a lot of work in with the chapel side and Joe Bailey was the Sunday School superintendent. Not to forget little Billy Hill who took the children for singing, preparing them for the annual anniversary, the charity day. On the morning of charity day we children would all meet at Sunday School and with the aid of a brass band would set to walk around the streets of the village singing songs and hymns. At about twelve o'clock we would return to Sunday School to be treated to ice buns cakes and drinks. In the afternoon at 2.30 and in the evening at 6.00 pm, the children would all go on to a stage which was built in the main chapel and would sing their hearts out to the delight of Mr Hill who had trained them. The evening collection would be taken and quickly counted and added to the morning and afternoon service collection and the amount raised would be announced by the minister.

Silverdale Pentecostal Church

Silverdale had a Pentecostal Church in Cross Street. It was small, but well run by Harry Weston and his family. Harry was the manager of the Silverdale Colliery canteen and hated swearing and bad behaviour, and it was amazing how people in his canteen respected the man and his Church beliefs. I believe that it was very rare for anyone to swear within Harry's earshot. The church had problems with the building in Cross Street, so they moved to the Rookery. It was named the Bethel Temple.

This continued under Harry's leadership for many years and when Harry passed away, it was taken on by Mr Proctor and his wife. Once again it was very successful with good attendance. When Mr. Proctor passed away the Bethel Temple was closed and sold to Silverdale Methodist church to be used as an additional room for various functions.

The Elim Pentecostal

The Elim Church was first opened in 1935 in Albert Street in an old shop converted to make this very small church. They continued there until 1980 when a lovely new church was built in High Street. The numbers grew so quickly that an extension was added in 1986. Shortly after, a second extension was built and now in 1998 a further extension is about to commence.

Then church hosts a very successful luncheon club for elderly people, a youth club choir, house groups and a very popular Sunday school. They have minibuses to collect and take people back home.

Pastor Williams arrived in Silverdale in 1970 with his wife Sue, who works with her husband. He is still going strong in 1998 but has an assistant now, Pastor Graham, who also lives on the village. Father Williams and Father Graham, Don Proctor and David Hough can be seen enjoying a game of golf on the municipal golf course a couple of mornings each week.

Part of the history of Silverdale, and a founder member of the Elim, Mr Ernest Rowley of Sneyd Terrace was an insurance agent all his working life. Always a smile and a kind word, he set his life upon his beloved Elim. Married for 66 years, he held every office in the church, from Sunday School superintendent to elder. He was also a long serving member of the St. John's Ambulance. What better epitaph than 'one of God's Gentlemen'. His wife is still living, being looked after in a local nursing home. The Church is still supported by his daughter Brenda and son-in-law Ralph, his grandson Philip and Philip's wife Ruth, continuing this family connection.

The Bethel, Church Street (Built in 1856)

Anyone who remembers the Bethel will be very aware who was in charge there! Two lovely lady teachers, Miss Florrie Morrall and her sister Chressie. Florrie taught music at Knutton Secondary School and Chressie taught at Knutton Junior School. For many years their real love was the Bethel. Tom Griffin, another stalwart, was the Sunday School Superintendent, who organised their Sunday School Anniversary for many years. The Bethel held some excellent musical evenings. The Messiah and other classics. Frank Edwards, a lovely tenor singer, performed many times with top class singers of the day. The Bethel also hosted the Youth Club Concert Party shows when they moved from the old "Board School". The Youth Club was very successful at the Bethel with the extra help and musical knowledge. This lovely building also had to be demolished due to lack of support and increasing costs. Does anyone know why the piano stool at the Bethel had five legs? Some say it gave "Morrall" support, Florrie being the pianist.

The Free Church, High Street (Closed 1962)

This Chapel, although smaller than the other three mentioned, was still run with great enthusiasm by the Balance family of Mill Street. This family put a lot of work and love into their Chapel. One remembers Joyce Brindley very well, who was a very dedicated organist and ran the Sunday School with help from Doris Woodcock from Knutton. They too had a very good musical side and their Anniversary was always up to the standard of the other three. Joyce unfortunately contacted T.B., which was a very serious illness in those times, and she never really recovered her health and strength after. The Chapel was converted to the new Methodist Church, which combined all the Chapels, in 1962. In 1981 this Church was closed and a newly built one opened in Earl Street which continues to this day.

The Congregational Church
The Congregational Church still stands between Albert Street and Victoria Street. This is still the original building, the only original one left apart from the Church of England. As was usual on the village one family took full responsibility for the running of the church and this was the Jones family. There was Joseph Jones the builders of excellent repute who built quite a lot of new houses on the village. Mr Harry Jones and his family also had this love and the family still has to this day the running of this church in their hands.

The Primitive Chapel
This chapel was built in 1864 and is situated on the High Street and the corner of Abbey Street, a lovely large building with a large Sunday School room and upstairs a room for a youth club. Unfortunately in the late 1970s falling attendances and maintenance costs caused it to close down and eventually it was demolished. This chapel was in the capable hands of Mr Joe Mothershaw and his family. Joe loved to sing and could be heard singing on his cement mixing machine in Phillips builders yard where he worked. Mr and Mrs Cornes and their two daughters Brenda and Margaret, two very talented musicians, organised the music side of the chapel. Brenda still assists with the organ to this day in the new Methodist Church in Earl Street.

The Organists
Arthur Bailey, born on Silverdale, a member of the Wesleyan Chapel, where his dad Joe was Superintendent. A real gentleman is Arthur, can anyone imagine his commitment to the Methodist movement - for fifty to sixty years, Sunday after Sunday, always there never letting the Chapel down. He still plays now at the new Methodist Chapel in Earl Street. His wife, Nellie, has always supported him in his love of music and the Chapel. I have spoken to a lot of Silverdale Methodists and everyone appreciates Arthur's dedication.

Harold Wilkinson, born in Silverdale in Church Street, where his dad was a shoe repairer. Harold again is a very accomplished organist and pianist. Harold used to play the organ in the Primitive Chapel until it was demolished in 1963. A friend of Arthur Bailey for many years, Harold will often step in to help out at the new Methodist if Arthur is indisposed. For many years Harold has played the organ at Audlem Methodist Church and Bridgemere Chapel at Woore. If any Chapel or Church is stuck you can bet Harold will do his best to help out. He plays for Newcastle Male Voice Choir Rehearsals if their pianist cannot get. He gets invited to play at weddings and funerals. A very committed Christian and nice person and everyone appreciates his dedication.

The Brylcreem Boys
on Charity Day

Dressed in Anniversary best.

Joe Bailey Sunday School
Superintendent at Sunday School
Anniversary.

United Methodist Free Church on the High Street. Demolished to make way for modern housing.

Bethel Temple a photograph taken just prior to its purchase by the Methodist Church

This old tin church, now demolished, stood across the road from the Primitive Methodist Chapel.

Congregational Church, Victoria Street - still standing.

The Salvation Army Band was based in Earl Street, just off Crown Street.

Silverdale Primitive Methodist Chapel Pantomime 1948-49

The Bethel Temple Church survived for many years. In 1995 the building was purchased by the Silverdale Methodist Church for use as an additional room.

Charity Sunday procession, just setting off from the Free Church on High Street.

The Bethel wedding of Sylvia Griffin, who married Wilf Spain. Tom Griffin is standing, left of the bride. Chrissie Morrall, middle row extreme left, Florrie Morrall second row extreme right. Wilf and Sylvia owned Bickley's Tool Shop in Bridge Street, Newcastle, which they ran until their retirement in 1997.

Chapel in the cemetery, soon to be demolished and reconstructed on a new site at Chatterley Mining Museum.

Anniversary Day with the Scout band leading the procession from Abbey Street and along Park Road, which was known to us as Back Lane.

Children walked around the village on the Chapel anniversary, singing to raise money for chapel funds.

Christmas Fair, 1970

Free Church Chapel Anniversary Sunday.

Interior, St Luke's Church, Silverdale

Church and Schools, Silverdale

St Luke's Church, Silverdale

St Luke's bells ready to be installed in 1907.

Sneyd Terrace in 1904.

The Bethel Church on the corner of Chapel Street and Church Street as it looked in the 1930s.

Elim Church originated in 1935 in this row of terraces in Albert Street and continued here until 1980. when a fine new church was built in High Street. The first extension was added in 1986. This was soon followed by a second extension.

Joe Mothershaw pictured during the Primitive Methodist Charity Day

Tom Griffin, Sunday School Superintendent at Bethel Methodist Church

Mr Ernest Rowley, who started the original church in Albert Street

Silverdale Roman Catholic Church, High Street

A council-built project nursing home for the elderley, Brighton House stands alongside St Luke's Church and has provided a wonderful facility for the village. It has an excellent reputation and the Friends of Brighton House have raised thousands of pounds for the home.

Chapter Eight
POLICE AND POLITICS 'ON THE DALE'

The Politicians

William (Bill) Nixon

Silverdale was a very lucky village to have a Labour councillor who devoted most of his spare time between 1949 and 1974 to the village. Bill was the elder of the Silverdale Councillors and saw the start of the redevelopment of the Church Street shops and Brook Street where he lived with his wife Fanny and his two sons, Eric and Brian.

The properties were demolished and Bill and his family moved to Underwood Road to a new house. This was a great move for Bill because it took him right by Silverdale Cricket Club, of which he was Chairman for a good many years. He very rarely missed matches - weekday or weekend.

He was an excellent employee of the PMT bus service and worked for them for 26 years. A very proud moment came for Bill when he was invited to be Mayor of the Borough in 1970. After doing an excellent job he was invited to continue for one more year, which he gladly accepted and once again did a very good job. I can remember most Tuesday evenings in the summer the Mayor's car would be parked at the rear of the cricket pavilion. This was selection night for the teams for the following weekend. Bill would not miss this meeting if at all possible and would have to dash off sometimes to go on a Mayoral engagement.

Bill and Fanny's two sons, Eric and Brian, went to Silverdale Infants and Junior School from where they both passed the 11 plus examination to Newcastle High School. From here Eric went on to Manchester University and after getting his degree he went on to London University as a professor of mathematics. Brian went from the High School to Oxford University and gained his degree in geography. Brian played cricket for Silverdale for many years before a knee injury forced him to retire.

Bill and Fanny were very proud of their sons' achievements and the sons were very proud of what their father achieved in his political and working life. Anyone who remembers Silverdale with all the old houses and smoky chimneys should look back and think, thank goodness for people like Bill Nixon, who put so much time and effort in. We can all see the wonderful changes that have taken place since Bill joined the Council in 1949. He retired from the Council in 1974 and passed away in January 1991. I knew Bill from when I was a boy until he died, cutting his hair for all these years and always found him to be a perfect gentleman.

Elsie Ashley

Elsie was born on Silverdale in one of the Brighton Cottages near to Silverdale Colliery and the nearby Railway Station. When she married, they moved to a small cottage on the High Street across from Sweetenham's shop. Eventually she went into business with Clewlows Timber, whose yard was on the Higher Land, Newcastle. She moved from Silverdale to live in the Westlands and took up an interest in politics in 1963, was selected to represent the Westlands Ward -- and won the seat. She carried on successfully taking part in County Council politics as well as the Borough Council.

In 1979 she was offered the honour of representing the Conservative Party, to stand for parliament against John Golding, Labour M.P. At this time, she nearly created quite a stir, when she only lost by a small majority of votes to take the seat. She carried on in local politics, and in 1993 she was thrilled to be invited to be Mayor of the Borough.

There had been some political ill feeling over the Mayoral post and it was generally thought

Elsie Ashley OBE JP M UNIV (Keele)
Freeman of the Borough of Newcastle-under-Lyme.
Mayor 1993-1994

Bill Hughes, Mayor
1986-87

Bill Nixon, Mayor
1970-71, 1971-72

that no Conservative would be asked to be Mayor again. All credit to the Labour party who were at the time being led by Mike Brereton. It was pointed out that Elsie really did deserve the honour. It was put to the vote and passed. During her term of office she did hundreds of engagements, justifying the faith of her fellow politicians.

In 1994 she decided to retire from politics and wind down after not being well. Sadly her husband Danny died and she now lives on her own but she is surrounded by lots of friends. Elsie will be remembered for her willingness to listen to people and always do her best to help them.

Derek Huckfield (Labour)

Born on Silverdale in Church Street Derek has been a Silverdale and Knutton Councillor for ten years. Derek, who has worked at Wedgwoods in Barlaston all his working life, is the union representative for the workers at the factory.

He joined Newcastle Council in 1988 and has done a very worthwhile job. Derek has been very involved with the Gypsy Site being moved from the Lyme Valley. It was decided by Staffordshire County Council in 1973 that the Gypsies would have to move from the Lyme Valley to another properly built site in Newcastle Borough. Silverdale area seemed to be the main target, with several sites being proposed but no one wanted them living near them so every time a site was mentioned Derek Huckfield, with his colleague Bill Hughes, were called to meetings on the village, which were packed to the doors with people protesters.

The first site earmarked in 1975 was Rosemary Hill Tile Works at Silverdale but this was dropped due to local opposition in 1977. Over the next twelve years six more sites were proposed but every site was squashed owing to different problems. But in 1990 Staffordshire County Council announced their plans for a site off Cemetery Road, near to Silverdale. The Evening Sentinel, Tuesday 29th May 1990, reported that Newcastle Council had no objection to this site and a meeting was called at Newcastle Council Offices at 7.00pm, with Bill Hughes inviting the public to make their views known. Protesters from Paris Avenue and Gallowstree Lane and Silverdale people made a valiant attempt to have this site stopped but it seemed the County Council were fed up of being thwarted at every proposal, so the Gypsies at last were to get their new site.

Bill Hughes

Bill joined Newcastle Borough Council as a Labour councillor in 1979 and has represented Silverdale in every election until now (1998). There is no doubt that he has been one of the best and hardest working councillors in the Borough. His passion for Silverdale is still as strong now as when he started in 1979.

To try to mention everything Bill has been involved in would take page after page so I will mention just a few. When Bill became a Ward Councillor street after street were very old terraced houses, no bathrooms, no indoor toilets, cellars full of water causing terribly damp conditions, wallpaper just peeled off with damp. People's health was suffering, with bronchitis, pneumonia, and other respiratory problems. Bill was horrified by the conditions and with the help of other Councillors they got things moving and the District Valuers and Health Department decided to totally redevelop all these streets.

Anyone coming on to the village now will see what Bill fought for. New houses, old folks bungalows, all with modern conveniences, comfortable and warm, and amid all this the Doctors' Surgery, a lovely new building with every facility for their patients. Brighton House with their bungalow scheme is another wonderful facility. Two new schools have been built, Silverdale Primary and Junior on the Racecourse and St. Luke's Primary and Junior in Pepper Street.

Bill's love of walking in the countryside means he keeps a watchful eye on public footpaths -

and makes sure they are kept open. He was very involved in getting a weight restriction on lorries passing through Silverdale village to the colliery. They were speeding through the village and making a lot of noise, particularly when they were empty. After a while the restriction order was granted and all lorries over a certain weight are banned, and this has been a great relief to the residents, especially the older people and children.

Bill has also managed to get safer roads by having police cameras set up at both ends of the village. His tireless work for the village and Borough Council and County Council committees brought him and his wife, Dorothy, the honour of being asked to be Mayor of Newcastle 1986-87.

Silverdale Church, of which Bill is in the choir and on the Church Committee, had a controversial period when mining subsidence affected the structure. The National Coal Board offered to repair the damage, or build a new modern church. The Committee were split on what to do; Bill favoured keeping the old church because it is such a lovely building. Eventually the old church was repaired and refurbished and still stands very proudly to the satisfaction of everyone.

One little story about Bill Hughes. I wonder how many people know that he was a professional footballer with Stoke City when he was a youth? One thing is certain, he is still as enthusiastic to this day about his love for Silverdale and keeps a very watchful eye on his beloved village and constituents.

Shock for Labour, 1969
During this period, Silverdale saw a lot of new development which lead to controversy in local politics. Michael Nicklin, a Silverdale boy, went into politics and fought hard for different projects but did not seem to be getting anywhere so he left the Labour Party and took up the Conservative banner. No one gave him a chance. Nevertheless in the Borough Elections of 1969 Michael became Conservative Councillor for Silverdale and proceeded to 'rock the boat' against Labour for a year or two. Eventually, in the next elections, he lost his seat to Labour again.

Silverdale Police

Silverdale Police Station
This was in Newcastle Street with its own cells for prisoners who were mainly "drunks". It was later sold to the Co-op and converted in to the workshop and garage where all the Co-op vehicles were sent for repairs. This was run by Reg Burgess a well known local mechanic. The new police station and police houses were built on High Street next to Harry Bonsall's petrol station.

Ray Hazel
In the 1940s Silverdale had its own police station in Newcastle Street opposite the Wesleyan Chapel.

It housed a sergeant and two constables who lived on the premises. One very well known policeman who came as Sergeant in 1943 was Ray Hazel who went on to have a very distinguished career, ending up as Chief Superintendent in Hanley. When he first came to live on Silverdale his accommodation was not ready so he came to live with my parents for a few weeks in our shop premises on Crown Street. He was a very good musician, pianist and organist so he made many many friends on and off the village with his musical talent.

Bill Roper
One of Sergeant Hazel's officers was Bill Roper whose local knowledge was invaluable. An excellent policeman, always cycling around the village keeping his eye on things, Bill's biggest asset was that people would call him over as he was passing and supply him with information so he was nearly always one step ahead of most criminals. In those days there were four boxes about six feet high with

a light on top. If the light was flashing the passing policeman would hop off his bike open the box and there was a phone inside where he could take any messages. Then, every two hours, the policeman would also phone in to the station at Newcastle to let them know that he was alright. If he did not ring in then someone would come out to see what was wrong.

Roy Ashley

A Silverdale lad who joined the police force in 1958 after leaving the Grenadier Guards. Six foot four, fifteen stones in weight, a very formidable character indeed and most local criminal 'tough types' did not tangle with Roy. He was a very nice person really and he worked on the village for six years with Bill Roper. In 1964 he moved to CID plainclothes and for the next twenty years had a very interesting and successful career. He finished his days working in the CID (Criminal Intelligence Department).

The Mayor and Mayoress with Michael Nicklin at a Bring and Buy Sale.

Brownies with Mayor

Lady Daleian's Choir 1962

Silverdale ladies inspecting the mace in the Mayor's parlour, closely watched by the Mayor and Mayoress,
Mr and Mrs Bill Nixon

Police post in front of the bus shelter.

P.C. (Sergeant) William Roper.

It was a sad day when these lovely cottages just below the church were demolished, to be replaced by modern flats.

Brookside - the house in which Joseph Cook was born. These properties were originally thatched. The picture was taken in 1937 just prior to demolition.

Chapter Nine
THE GOOD OLD DAYS

Back Lane Spring

Back Lane was the road that ran from the top of High Street through to the Keele Road. It was a narrow lane with passing spaces for cars but when the new Cemetery Road was built it became very quiet. Some Gypsy families began to use it making life difficult for walkers and cyclists, especially because their dogs were constantly having a go at people. Eventually the council blocked the lane off to through traffic by putting steel barriers across it, and it is now a pleasant walk for the villagers.

The spring runs from somewhere in Keele, down through the fields to a concrete trough on Park Lane. When we were kids we drank gallons of this icy cold water scooping it up in our hands. On Sunday mornings, local footballers would go and sit with their injured ankles, arms or legs immersing them in the ice cold water. Swellings would visibly disappear and most of them would be playing the following week! It is interesting to note that a 'modern' method of treating sports injuries is ice packs.

A few years ago the water authority put a ban on drinking the water out of the trough because of its iron content, but it still runs as clear as it did 50 years ago. With the modern fertilisers and pesticides the farmers put on their fields nowadays it is probably a sensible thing not to drink it.

The Good Old Days

> We met and we married a long time ago,
> We worked long hours when wages were low,
> No television, wireless or baths, times were hard
> Just cold water taps, and a walk in the yard,
> No holidays abroad or posh carpets on the floors,
> But we had a coal fire, and we didn't lock doors,
> Our children arrived and a real home we made,
> And we brought them all up without State Aid,
> They were always quite safe to play in the park,
> That's when old people could go out in the dark,
> No vandals, no mugging, there was nothing to rob,
> We all felt quite rich with a couple of bob,
> Milkmen and Paperboys would whistle and sing,
> A night at the pictures was having a fling,
> We got our full share of trouble and strife,
> But we just had to face it, it was the pattern of life,
> Now I'm alone, I look back through the years,
> I don't think of the hard times, the trouble or tears,
> I remember the blessings, our home and our love,
> We shared them together, and thanked God above.

George Valco

Mr Green, Night Soil Remover

What a Job! Who remembers the miserable Mr Green who went from house to house removing and emptying the tin drum which fitted under the wooden seat in the toilet, usually in a separate little brick built shed in the backyard? His horse and cart had a large container to empty the toilet contents into. Local lads used to call him names and laugh at him and he would threaten what he would do for them if he caught them.

One day, when he was returning the tin drum to one house, the boys quickly slipped the straps

Back Lane Spring, still running to this day and never known to stop, not even in 1976, the
year of the great drought.

Poole's bus stopping on Park Site.

undone on his horse's shafts and ran off to hide. Mr. Green returned and told the horse to move forward, the horse did so and suddenly the shafts shot up in the air and the container came rolling off the back of the cart, throwing its smelly load on to the road.

Suddenly all one could hear was a succession of bangs, one after the other, as people banged their windows closed because of the smell. The boys thought it was hilarious. Mr Green was not so pleased and had to spend a few hours, with the help of neighbours, washing the awful mess away. The boys kept a very low profile where Mr Green was concerned for quite a while after this incident.

Outside Toilets

John Tye lived with his family in one of the terraced houses next door to the Wheatsheaf Pub, now called The Silver Birch. Their toilet was at the top of the yard right by the railway line, and when a train came past you had to hold on to the seat because of the heavy vibration. As you sat there your body shook to the rhythm of the train on the line.

Most outside toilets in the winter had a small parrafin lamp hanging on a piece of wire just under the cold water cistern to try and stop it from freezing. The smell of parrafin fumes made sure you did not stay any longer than required. And there was no fancy soft toilet paper; it was the Sentinel or morning newspaper cut into quarter size pieces and hanging on a piece of string.

Mr. George Jackson, who now lives in Newcastle, tells me the story of the old gothic cottages which backed on to the railway line in Church Street. All the cottages had the toilet up the backyard. The local lads used to wait on the railway line until it was dark, when the back door would open and one of the men came out carrying a candle and go in to the toilet. They would give him a minute or two to sit down on and then throw bricks and coal onto the tin roof of the toilet. The door would fly open and the man would shout at the boys to clear off but they just stood and laughed, as he stood there with his trousers round his ankles.

Public Transport and Duggin's Bus Service

Silverdale was served by the Potteries Electric Traction (P.E.T.) trams between Silverdale and Newcastle. The driving platform was open and the drivers were exposed to all weathers. The trams went up the High Street to the terminus at the Bush, returning via Church Sreet and Newcastle Street. At the Bush the conductor would remove the pole from the overhead cable by means of a attached rope. He would walk to the other end of the tram and swivel the pole onto the overhead cable at the rear keeping the pole always in the trailing position. The rails were in large square set stones flush with the road with tar between them. In cold temperatures it went very hard but in warm weather the tar became soft and stuck to the soles of your clogs or boots. At the time of the picture P.E.T. Tramcars were in fierce competition from other passenger carrying vehicles.

The first to operate this route was a firm called Cornes. Then Birkin and Rutter, later on these became Dean and Holdcroft and later still Pooles. The service down Church Street to Newcastle was run by Garbett and Bonett and "Duggins" Princess Bus Service. This competition soon proved the end of the tramcars and they were withdrawn in 1928. The P.E.T. substituted buses and then the fierce competition was ended when a licensing authority was set up in Birmingham controlling the whole West Midlands area. This removed competition as no unauthorised vehicles were able to operate.

Duggin's bus service ran on Silverdale for about 40 years. The owner Irene Duggins lived in May Bank on the outskirts of Newcastle. She employed two crews of a driver and conductor, Edgar Dean and Ernie Peake on one shift, and Jim Turner and Eric Mothershaw on the other, with Jim Turner's wife as stand-in conductor for both shifts. They had one bus which was locally called the 'Matchbox'. It officially carried 28 people but could be seen at peak times carrying twice as many as that, with as many standing as seated.

Outside closets - once a typical back yard scene - mostly now demolished.

Madeley Street looking towards High Street.

When the 'Matchbox' had had its days, a lovely new maroon bus took its place. What a difference for comfort this was. This was a 50 seater but once again they would load seventy to eighty people on board to save leaving any passengers behind. The conductors used to hand punch the tickets with a ticket machine which produced little coloured circles. .People would ask the conductor for these to use as confetti at weddings.

This excellent service went out of business when Mrs Duggins sold out to the P.M.T. - and Ernie, Eric, Edgar, Jim and Mrs Turner were nearing retirement.

Having a bet!

This was against the law except with registered bookmakers, but most bookies had 'runners' who collected bets. One named Tommy Wright seemed to do the bottom of the village. I remember once Tommy was caught by the police. The plain clothes police had a car with the bonnet up pretending to be broken down but all the time they were watching Tommy come down Church street collecting his bets at people's front doors. He was caught red-handed, was arrested and later fined.

The other bookie's runner at the top of the village was Mary Ann Dale, wife of Jack Dale. Mary Ann used her house for people to come and lay bets on. People brought their bets to her and sometimes watched the race on television., sitting in her house, having a chat and a bet. One Saturday afternoon panic broke out when the police black maria van swooped down on the house and arrested 10 people. They all had to appear in court and were fined ten shillings each.

Mary Anne was fined a lot more than this but as soon as the case was over it was back to business as usual! "Get your bets on lads." Mary Anne was a real village character with a great sense of humour. The bookmaker she worked for was Ken Slack, who retired and sold out to Tommy Nee who opened the first betting shop in the village. He moved on and Warren Brookes now provides the service in the High Street.

The Monkey Run

Can anyone remember the monkey run on Silverdale where the boys and girls used to walk up and down on Saturday and Sunday evenings. The walk went from the bridge at the bottom of Armitages Bank up to Red Heath House and round the path to the old colliery offices at the top of the Treacle Row, back down to the bridge and then round again.

Black People

The first two black people who came to live on the village were named Andy, a Nigerian, and Fabian from Biafra. They came to work and learn with the electricians and technical staff at the colliery. They lived with Mr and Mrs Trotter, two lovely Silverdale people. They turned out to be very pleasant professional young men, especially considering their two countries were at war at the time. Both went on to have successful careers.

Silverdale: New Era of Private Houses

1952-1953: The Park Site Estate was built on top of the hill from the Treacle Row to Hollywood. It was built in two styles; brick and tile houses and new concrete sectional designs. This was the start of a new era for the area. The 'Geordies' began to arrive to work in the mines. The Coal Board had closed a lot of pits up in the North-East and these people had to up roots and come to live here. When they arrived no one could tell a word they said and they must have felt really out of place. Gradually they began to settle down and live in the Park Site community.

On Park Site was a large old house, which at one time was the Old Colliery House owned by the Cocks family, owners of the Colliery. The Cocks family sold the house to Ridgways, the family who had a music store in Hanley for many years. The new community were finding it difficult to settle to the pubs and clubs on the old village so a consortium of Silverdale business men secured a lease on Silverdale House and in 1955, with the help of a brewery, converted it to a working men's club. The club was very successful and the members and committee bought the lease from the consortium through a shares system. It was very busy with good bingo houses which encouraged the village people to go along and have a drink, helping further to integrate the new community. This club is still going well today.

Birchall's Farm had been farmed for many years as a thriving concern, employing seven days a week, Teddy Hill, Ben Clegg, Jim Gorton, Gordon Birchall, Mr Birchall, and odd job man Len Peak. Silverdale Cricket Club was next to the farm. The farm was on very good ground with cornfields, hay, vegetable crops and grazing land for the milking cows. The colliery carnival was held every year on the Cricket Ground and horse jumping competitions were held on the fields at the rear of the Ground. This brought hundreds of cars and vans to park on the field and was a big thing for the village. In the mid-sixties Fletcher's builders bought a lot of the land and built 300 houses and bungalows which sold very quickly indeed. The Council then started the golf course project on the land and this opened as a full 18-hole course, club house, pub and golf shop in 1974.

Both the housing project and the golf course are a tremendous success and now the golf course is really beginning to mature, it can compete with any private course. It also has an excellent 26 bay driving range and there is talk by the Council of making a 9-hole course as an additional facility.

The Shelton Men: Subsidence Division

These men were responsible for the subsidence repairs caused by Silverdale Colliery all over the village. It was always 'the Shelton men are coming in'. They came to knock out ceilings, mend cracks in walls, door frames, floors and windows. When you saw them they were always coal black, faces and clothes, from the dust they worked in. It was amazing but they never seemed to get ill. There was Tommy Goodwin, foreman from Clayton; Ted Ray, joiner from Crackley Gates Scot Hay; Joe Ankers, labourer from Black Bank; Tom Myatt, labourer from Silverdale, and Ern Ward of Church Street. They were a great team of men, always busy on one house after the other.

One time in the 1950s Kinsey Street was partly evacuated because of the state of the houses. You could walk in at the side of the front doors, the gaps in the brickwork were so big. Entry doors were jammed solid and could not be opened in fear of collapse. The people living in these houses were moved to Clayton on to a new estate and returned home months later when repairs were complete. The ceilings in those old terraced houses were lath and plaster, so one can imagine the dust and dirt, but eventually everyone returned home to their homes fully repaired and decorated. These men were experts in their field and did a wonderful job of the repairs.

Foreign troops

Mrs Oakes of Silverdale was telling me about the French troops stationed at Trentham Gardens during World War II, who decided to look a bit further afield for girlfriends and arrived in Silverdale. They were all bronzed and good looking with berets and long cloaks - it was quite a culture shock for Silverdale mothers and fathers to see them hold their cloaks open and 'wee' in the street. They quickly ran out to fetch their daughters off the street because of what they would see. Apparently the soldiers wondered what was going on because in France this was what they always did. Even today they are certainly less inhibited than the British - but when you think of Silverdale in the 1940s!!

Another little story told to me was about when the American troops were stationed at Keele,and they used Spooners Dance Hall a lot so they obviously knew many of the girls on the village. Their favourite courting spot was the Jolly's playing fields. The local boys would very carefully follow discreetly and watch where they went. Just like commandos in the army they would crawl through the grass until they could see what was going on, suddenly they would shout out and the couple would jump up wondering what was happening. The American would try and run after them but the boys knew he could not catch them with his trousers round his ankles.

Evacuees

Many evacuees who came from London to live on Silverdale during the War remained on the village afterwards, having settled in the community. The Piggott family lived in Kinsey Street. Mr Piggott Senior worked for many years at Newcast Foundry in Cemetery Road. Two of his sons worked in Silverdale Colliery and the third son George was a painter and decorator with Newcastle Council. The sons still live in Silverdale. The Birch family lived in Albert Street, both father and son working at G.E.C. Milehouse until they retired. The Tye family lived in Church Street, next to the Wheatsheaf pub. The family still live in the Newcastle area, Mr Tye Senior in an old folks bungalow scheme in Clayton and his sons, John, Patrick and Robert and daughter Eileen in the Newcastle area.

A large Polish contingent moved in to Silverdale, to Parksite Estate, to work in the colliery. They lived in Donington, Shropshire, and came by bus every day to the colliery. They were very hard working people, who settled in and made a good life for their families.

Belisha beacon

Dan Hough, who attended Silverdale Schools as a boy, informs me that the first flashing Belisha beacon was installed outside Silverdale Board School in 1936. All the children were led from school to be told how it worked and told that cars must stop when children were waiting to cross. This encouraged the children to walk across and then come straight back again making the cars wait - a little game which soon stopped when they realised they would be in trouble.

Crown Bank - New co-op offices

Earl Street, with the Salvation Army headquarters on the right.

Albert Street. Braddock's Bakery was here on the right. When it closed in the 1960s it was converted to make fireplaces by Jack Lawrence who ran quite a successful business here for many years.

Abbey Street. Farmer's Bank goes off to the left with Finnemore's bungalow just beyond it which was also a small shop selling sweets, confectionery and cigarettes.

The new Police houses and the Police station can be seen on the right. Mr Fred Davies, Sergeant took over the new Police Station about 1970 and was assisted by Constable Brian Dean and Constable David Owen

Crown Bank. The Coop main offices were situated at the top of this street with the Coop furniture store on the corner of Victoria Street off it. With a variety of small shops this area was always busy. In pre-War days Crown Bank was used by politicians to address meetings.

Kinsey Street. These houses were hit by severe subsidence in the early 1950s and residents had to move out to a new estate in Clayton while their properties were repaired.

Earl Street. Tennis courts, a bowling green and a new doctors surgery are here now.

Cottages in the High Street which are still standing.

Downing Street c1900
All these lovely old cottages have been demolished to make way for modern houseing.

Another view of Downing Street c1900.

Brook Street was demolished when the redevelopment of the Church Street shops began, because this row of houses backed on to Church Street. This area is now part of the new park, tennis courts and bowling green.

Abbey Street still looks exactly the same in 1998 - it is hoped that this street will be conserved.

Silverdale House. This large house in extensive grounds was occupied by the Cadman Family from 1887 to about 1930. It was then used by the Silverdale Colliery Manager Mr D H Cocks until somewhere in the early 1940s. It was then sold on to the Ridgway family of the well-known music shop in Hanley. When they left in 1953 it stood empty until it became a working men's club for the Park Site Estate and still remains so.

Redheath House, Pepper Street, Silverdale, the original home of Captain Goodwin

LOT 34
(Coloured Lt. Green on Plan No. 1)

THE CONVENIENTLY SITUATED DAIRYING AND MIXED HOLDING

SILVERDALE FARM

SILVERDALE

Area : 157 a. 1 r. 16 p.

Tenancies

Tenant	Description	Acreage	Annual Rent	Tenancy
Mr. A. Birchall	Silverdale Farm and 1 Cottage	154.783	£253 6 8	Yearly Lady Day
In Hand	Woodlands	2.567	—	—
		157.350	£253 6 8	

The House

is situated adjacent to the Farm premises, and forms the end house of the residential block known as " Sneyd Villas ", High Street, Silverdale, and is equipped with all modern conveniences.

Construction : Brick and tile.

Accommodation : Hall, Drawing Room, Dining Room, Kitchen with range and cupboards, Pantry, Scullery with sink (h. & c.), 3 Bedrooms, Bathroom with Bath (h. & c.), basin (h. & c.) and airing cupboard, separate W.C. and Boxroom.

Outside : Coal Place, Shed and W.C.

Main Water, Electricity and Gas and Main Drainage

Farm Premises

brick and tile built

comprising :

Dairy, Mess Room ; **Cowhouse with tyings for 34 cows** with tubular divisions, concrete floor and standings, and railed feeding passage, Fodder Place, Double **Cowhouse with tyings for 20 cows**, similarly equipped, but without feeding passage ; 5 Calves Boxes or Piggeries with Loft over one ; Loose Box ; Turnip House, Mixing Place ; Large Loose Box ; 3 Loose Boxes and 3 Stall Stable with Loft Over ; Storage Barn with Loft over, 2 Tractor Sheds and old Engine House. Dutch Barns, 11 Bays.

Water Supply to Farm Premises from Silverdale Spring Pool Supply
(See Note 2 below)

Cottage

being one of a pair of brick and tile built Cottages known as " Butts Cottages " situated between Lots 12 and 18 and containing Sitting Room, Kitchen, Pantry and 2 Bedrooms.

Outside : Coal Place and Shed. E.C.

Water from Pump.

Landlord pays Rates—Rateable Value £7.

LOT 58
(Coloured Red on Plan No. 1)
The

Conservative Club Premises

WITH LIVING ACCOMMODATION

Church Street, Silverdale

Let on Yearly Tenancy to the Silverdale Conservative Club at a rent of £25 0s. 0d. a year (Tenants paying Rates.)

Area : 13 perches (approx.)

(Pt. Ord. No. 424, Newcastle-under-Lyme—1937 Edition.)
The Property is built of brick and tile and contains the following accommodation :

Ground Floor : Hall, Club Room, Reading Room and Smoke Room, W.C., Bar, Store Place, Sitting Room, Scullery, Pantry.

First Floor : Toilet Room and W.C., Billiards Room ; 3 Bedrooms.

Outside : Washhouse with copper, Coal Place and W.C., Fuel and Store Sheds.

Main Water, Gas and Electricity Supplies

NOTE

The Central Heating system and Boiler, Cooking Range and domestic hot water system, and all fittings in connection with the occupation of the property as Club Premises have been installed at the Tenants' expense.

LOT 59
(Coloured Brown on Plan No .1)

THE EXCEPTIONALLY ATTRACTIVE RESIDENTIAL PROPERTY

REDHEATH HOUSE

SILVERDALE

with Garden and Grounds of approximately

2 a. 1 r. 5 p.

(Ord. Nos. 128 and Pt. 137, Keele—1924 Edition.)

As let on Yearly Tenancy to Mr. J. H. Ramsbotham at a rent of

£70 : 0 : 0 a year

(Tenant paying Rates).

The House, which is substantially built of brick with a tiled roof, is approached by a semi-circular gravelled sweep, and is screened from the road by trees and shrubs.

It contains the following accommodation :—

On the Ground Floor :
Porch, Hall, Dining Room with tiled fireplace, Drawing Room with bay window and tiled fireplace, Sitting Room with tiled fireplace, Butlers Pantry with cupboards and sink (h. & c.), Kitchen with range (with boiler for domestic hot water supply), and cupboards, Pantry, Scullery with sink (h. & c.), Cellar.

On the First Floor : (approached by two staircases)
3 principal Bedrooms, 2 secondary Bedrooms and Dressing Room, Bathroom with bath (h. & c.) and basin (h. & c.), separate W.C., Linen Cupboard.

Outside :
Back Yard with former Washhouse, Coal Place and Wood Store, Garden Store Shed.

Main Water and Gas Supplies

The Garden and Grounds

have been delightfully laid out and exceptionally well maintained. They form a most attractive feature of the property and comprise lawns, flower beds, trees and shrubberies, sloping down to a Pond.

Outgoings
Tithe Redemption Annuities £0 5s. 9d. (apportioned)

NOTES
1. The Tenant claims the timber built Garage and the 2 Greenhouses.
2. All appointments to inspect this property must be arranged direct with the Tenant.

LOT 86A
(Coloured Brown on Plan No. 3)

The semi-detached stone and tile built

" GATESIDE COTTAGE "

with Garden, Keele

Area : 31 Perches (approx.)
(Pt. Ord. No. 38, Keele—1937 Edition.)

Tenant : Mrs. Askey.
Rent : £12 0s. 0d. a year (Tenant paying Rates).
Tenancy : Yearly.

The Cottage contains :

Sitting Room with range and cupboards ; Kitchen with sink ; 2 Bedrooms.

Outside : Washhouse with copper and sink ; 2 Pig Styes and E.C. ; lean-to timber and iron Coal Place.

Gas Supply. Water Supply—see General Remarks and Stipulations No. 14.

NOTES

This Lot is sold
(a) with the benefit of a right of way for access thereto as now used over the adjoining Gateside Cottage property retained by the Vendors.
(b) subject to rights of way as now used reserved for the benefit of the Vendors' adjoining Gateside Cottage property for access to the E.C. and to steps leading to a Loft included in the said Cottage property of the Vendors.

LOT 87
(Coloured Blue on Plan No. 1)

A semi-detached

Cottage with Garden

BACK LANE, SILVERDALE

Area : 34 Perches (approx.)
(Pt. Ord. No. 513, Newcastle-under-Lyme—1937 Edition.)

Construction : Brick and tile.

Accommodation : Porch, Living Room with range, Sitting Room, Pantry ; 3 Bedrooms.

Outside : Washhouse with copper and sink, E.C. and Coal Place.

Water from adjacent Spring Supply
(See General Remarks and Stipulations No. 14.)

Let on Yearly Tenancy to Mr. P. Liner at a rent of £10 8s. 0d. a year (Tenant paying Rates).

NOTES
1. The Tenant claims : Cooking range in Living Room, tiled fireplace in Sitting Room, provision of boiler in copper, and the remainder of the buildings on this Lot.
2. As to Park Road for Back Lane) Silverdale—see General Remarks and Stipulations No. 15.

LOT 88
(Coloured Brown on Plan No. 1)

The Adjoining semi-detached brick and tile built

Cottage with Garden

BACK LANE, SILVERDALE

Area : 34 Perches (approx.)
(Pt. Ord. No. 513 and 514, Newcastle-under-Lyme—1937 Edition.)

Accommodation : Porch, Sitting Room, Living Room with range, Pantry ; 2 Bedrooms and Boxroom.

Outside : Scullery with sink, E.C., Store Shed.

Water from adjacent Spring Supply
(See General Remarks and Stipulations No. 14).

Let on Yearly Tenancy to Mr. D. Myatt at a rent of £10 0s. 0d. a year (Landlord paying Rates).

Rateable Value £5.

NOTES
1. The Greenhouse on this Lot is claimed by the Tenant.
2. As to Park Road for Back Lane) Silverdale—see General Remarks and Stipulations No. 15.

LOT 89
(Coloured Red on Plan No. 3)

A brick and tile built

Cottage with Garden

BACK LANE, SILVERDALE

Area : 12 Perches (approx.)
(Pt. Ord. No. 476, Newcastle-under-Lyme—1937 Edition.)

Accommodation : Living Room with range, Kitchen, Pantry ; 2 Bedrooms.

Outside : Coal Place, Pig Stye and E.C.

Let on Yearly Tenancy to Mrs. Ford at a rent of £5 4s. 0d. a year (Landlord paying Rates).

Rateable Value £5.

Outgoings
Tithe Redemption Annuities 2d. (apportioned)

NOTES
1. This Lot is sold with the benefit of all rights of way at present used over Lot 91 for access to the Cottage, Garden and Outbuildings on this Lot.

Another aspect of Abbey Street

Underwood Road, Silverdale

The Villas, High Street. The centre villa was occupied by Frank Allen, Colliery Manager at Silverdale from the 1950s to the 1970s. The villa on the right was the Vicarage for St Lukes until 1982.

Buxton Avenue, leading to Park Site, built in 1952

Duggin's bus.

Ern Hubbard and his horse, delivering the milk.

Park Road from the top of the meadow, showing the new development of houses and bungalows.

1970s development on High Street

Derelict land, Five Lane Ends - this particular corner had five streets running off it. The Working Men's Club
stood on this site, prior to relocating to High Street.

Cleared ground

Chapter Ten
INDUSTRY 'ON THE DALE'

Silverdale Colliery

In 1971 the colliery was the toast of the Common Market, with a colliery record of 1747 cwt per man shift which still stands to this day. In 1975 the Silverdale community was given a wonderful boost in the form of a 20 million pound investment in the colliery to open a new drift mine. This started in May 1976 and would have taken them easily into the next century. The Coal Authority purchased Redfern's Farm, which adjoined the colliery to expand into the fields. After a few early problems the colliery began to do well but then geological problems began to arise causing concern.

In 1993 Silverdale Colliery was forced to close, many say mainly due to politics and not geology. But it was a very sad day for all the families employed and for the local shops and businesses also affected. The colliery remained under care and maintenance by British Coal with about 30 men keeping watch on safety. When it was put up for sale, a firm called Coal Investments Ltd purchased the colliery and reopened it with 150 men keeping their jobs.

This went along very well, selling all the coal they could produce. But once again the colliery is due to close in December 1998. This time it really looks doomed and as one can read from the accompanying headlines that this looks like the end of the road for a business which started right back on April 6th 1792. The excellent monument and memorial plaque on the entry to the village at Stonewall is a fine tribute to the people who worked at Silverdale's "Kent's Lane".

Kent's Lane Colliery, Silverdale

Sadly by the time this book is published, Silverdale Colliery will be closed. December 31st 1998 will be the end of an era for North Staffordshire coal mining. Hopefully something good for Silverdale may come from it; according to the Evening Sentinel a task force has been set up to draw plans for the 180 acre site, to combine industry and commmerce.Perhaps the outcome will be decent employment and successful futures for the children of Silverdale miners.

The first pit closure was in 1957 of the Madeley (Leycett) Mine.Then followed a long list and Silverdale is the last:

1957	Madeley (Lycett)	1969	Stafford
1960	Berry Hill, Fenton	1969	Apedale Newcastle
1960	Glass House, Chesterton	1977	Chatterley Whitfield
1962	Parkhall, Longton	1977	Norton
1962	Hanley Deeppit	1982	Victoria Biddulph
1962	Sneyd Hanley	1983	Wolstanton
1963	Mossfield Longton	1989	Holditch Newcastle
1963	Kemball Heron Cross	1990	Lea Hall Rugeley
1964	Glebe Fenton	1993	Littleton Cannock
1965	Foxfield	1996	Hem Heath Trentham
1969	Parkhouse Chesterton	1998	Silverdale

Silverdale Railway Station

This was a busy place in the 1940s-50s. It had two platforms, one up and one down, porters' room, booking office, waiting room and toilets.There was a resident station master, Mr Peake who lived in a large house near to the station. There were porters, booking clerks and goods staff. Just below the station was a level crossing on Station Road with large road gates, operated manually by the signal box staff, and a wicket gate for pedestrians. The signal box was manned night and day. Further down the line was Crown Bank Halt where passengers were picked up and where Matthew Redfern used to cross the line from his farm to the village to deliver his milk. .

There was a goods depot with large storage sheds, and running alongside Silverdale Colliery, there were sidings for loading coal onto coal trucks for delivering coal all over the Country. Trains ran every day to Wedgwood's at Barlaston where a lot of Silverdale people worked. They also ran trains to Stoke City home matches, which were very well supported. One very well remembered tragedy was a young lady called Pat Shaw who was running to catch her train to Wedgwood's, slipped as the train was moving, and fell between the foot rail of the train and the platform. She lost both of her legs. The Railway line was closed to passengers in 1956 but still runs to this day for Silverdale Colliery. At this moment in time, Silverdale Railway Station is being taken down brick by brick and transferred to the Chatterley Mining Museum, where it will be rebuilt.

Belstaff Factory, High Street

This was opened in 1953, making waterproof coats and jackets and was a very successful company which employed mainly women. Eventually it moved to a new Industrial Estate in 1966 at Stonewall and was for a long time the most modern clothing factory in the Stoke on Trent area. In the 70s and 80s they were exporting Belstaff motorcycle clothing to 21 countries around the world especially North America but as far apart as Japan and Venezuela. In 1974, to meet the growing demand they opened two new factories in the North East. Things went very well and they expanded in to fishing and walking gear, supplying Britain's Ryder Cup Golf Team with their smart waterproof golf suits which were seen on television and became a very popular seller.

Things carried on successfully until 1990 when the recession hit the company very hard and they had to make people redundant, eventually closing down altogether with the loss of village jobs.

Newcast Foundry

This foundry was sited on Cemetery Road next to the Silverdale Cemetery and employed 120 men in very hot and smelly conditions. It was very successful for years until it had eventually to close down due to lack of orders.

Whalleys Brickyard, Opposite the Foundry

It is hard to imagine which had the worst working conditions, Whalleys who made hand made tiles or the foundry. Whalleys had excellent craftsmen who worked very long hours. It had its own marl pit ridge alongside the brick works. The chimneys piped thick smoke out all day long and when the doors of the mushroom shaped baking ovens were opened the burning flames glowed red and gave out the hot choking smell of the baking tiles. Whalleys was taken over by G.H. Downing and all tile making was transferred to a modern oven system heated by gas at the Knutton and Madeley sites. The marl hole is still in the same place today and the marl is taken by lorry to the various sites for production.

Silverdale Stonewall Industrial Estate

In an effort to clean up Silverdale village, Newcastle Council decided to open this site. At first most small businesses were reluctant to move from their present sites because of the expense of rents and rates and fitting out the premises with equipment. Eventually one or two firms moved down there. Belstaff, Stan Brunt (Rolls Royce specialist), Roberts' Transport, Roger's Coalyard. The site was eventually filled with small businesses and Silverdale Caravans. Most are still there today and although Belstaff closed a joinery firm has now taken over their unit.

Blacksmith Green and Blacksmith Fenton

Up until the late 1940s and early 1950s Silverdale had two blacksmiths, Mr Green who was next to the Roxy Cinema and Mr Fenton whose business was on the corner of Farmer's Bank and Abbey St. There were many working horses around that period so these blacksmiths were very busy. A blacksmith shoeing horses was a wonderful art and we stood hours watching the horses have their shoes fitted. As children, we could never work out why, when putting red hot shoes onto horses' feet and then knocking half a dozen nails into each foot, the horse just stood there with no apparent discomfort. It was very hard work for the farrier who had to wear a heavy apron and hold horses' legs between his own all day.

One little thing they would do for children was make us a bowler for sixpence. What was a bowler? The blacksmith had long pieces of half inch steel and would cut a piece off the length, warm it up on the anvil, put it into his large vice and make it into a circle, weld the two ends together, and that was your bowler. We would then get a stick of wood and have races down Crown Bank rolling the bowler with the stick.

With the advent of farm tractors and lorries these people have now become virtually extinct. At the end of Mr Green's smithy was Mr Ball who was a wheelwright. He was another expert to watch making wooden wheels and putting the iron rim around the wheel with amazing skill. The strength of the man alone to handle wood like he did, making different shapes and sizes for his customers. Wheels were made for haycarts, milk floats, and the odd pony trotting carts which were smaller and thinner. Mr Ball passed away many years ago but his daughter Selina still lives on the village in Dale View on the new estate off Park Road.

Silverdale Minerals, Chapel Street

A bottling store and amongst the many things bottled there was a variety of coloured mineral drinks in bottles with the old glass stopper. These bottles were first filled with minerals and then put onto a machine which inverted the bottle introduced gas and thus sealed the bottle by holding the glass marble in position by pressure. The opener for these bottles was a small wooden cylinder with a wooden peg in the centre. You placed the cylinder on top of the bottle with the peg in the neck and gave the cylinder a sharp blow with your hand and bingo the bottle was open.

The Mine Memorial was presented when the mine was closed. It was erected at
Stonewall, at the entrance to the village.

Part of the 1940 film, 'The Proud Valley' was shot on location at the colliery in Silverdale and George Bytheway, who worked in the Lamp Room, acted as stand-in for Paul Robeson and was filmed from the rear, walking up the tip.

Group of Silverdale Colliery Fitters

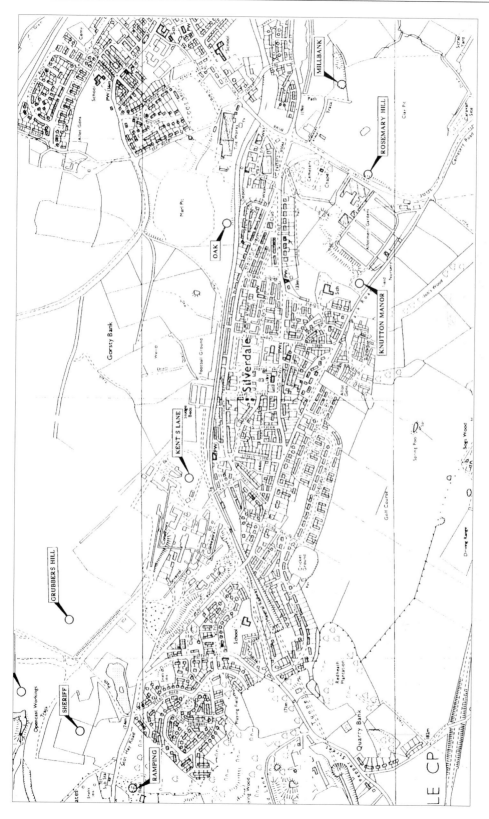

Some of the Silverdale Mines

Silverdale Big Pit No. 6 Colliery with the head gear of the older Sheriff Pit on the right.

Kents Lane Colliery

Pit Boys at start of a shift waiting for the cage.

Silverdale Colliery.

Silverdale - the end of an era

Taking down the headsticks.

Staffordshire pit closures

Madeley, 1957.
Berry Hill, Fenton, 1960.
Glasshouse, Chesterton, 1960.
Parkhall, Longton, 1962.
Hanley Deep Pit, 1962.
Sneyd, Hanley, 1962.
Mossfield, Longton, 1963.
Kemball, Heron Cross, 1963.
Glebe, Fenton, 1964.
Foxfield, 1965.
Parkhouse, Chesterton, 1969.
Stafford, 1969.
Apedale, Newcastle, 1969.
Chatterley Whitfield, 1977.
Norton, 1977.
Victoria, Biddulph, 1982.
Wolstanton, 1985.
Holditch, Newcastle, 1989.
Lea Hall, Rugeley, 1990.
Littleton, Cannock, 1993
Hem Heath, Trentham, 1996.
Silverdale, 1998

Action plan for doomed colliery site

Winners of the Rescue and First Aid competition

Arthur Shipley, aged 83, spent all his working life at Silverdale Colliery. The wooden seat behind him is where Arthur, Jim McGing, Albert Whalley and Bill Furmston spent many happy hours.

John Belcher retires from Silverdale Pit

●High Commissioner Mr Neal Blewett with Silverdale miners at the unveiling ceremony.

The first colliery train

The spoil heap, with the coliery on the left. In the foreground can be seen the railway crossing control, to the right of which are the Brighton Cottages.

Installation of electricity at Silverdale Colliery, 1918

1950s - Charles Brayford's retirement and send-off from Silverdale Colliery. Receiving a gift from Mr Jim Beardmore, Colliery Engineer.

A Silverdale pit pony, 1910

Park Site Club, originally the home of colliery manager D H Cocks and now the Working Men's Club.

Spring Pool, which was pumped from Silverdale Pit, was situated on the Golf Course at Keele and is now empty and overgrown.

Phillips Bros Builders, May Street.
This small building firm had an excellent reputation. It was run by Enoch Phillips and his brother, Richard. Enoch looked after the building side on site, checking that all was going well. Richard ran the wood workshop and maintained all the machinery. The brothers only employed the best workers and trained their own apprentices to a high standard.

New industrial site at Stonewall 1957.

Whalley's Tileries on Cemetery Road. Now demolished. All that remains is a marl hole.

Silverdale Road heading towards Newcastle, showing the crane removing the old bridge after the closure of the railway line.

One of the last steam trains to leave Silverdale Colliery

Silverdale tunnel. Silverdale Station below, showing the Colliery coal bunker to the right. Trains loaded coal here and continued through the tunnel above onto the Main Crewe line.

Last of the three large Foundry chimneys to be demolished at Knutton Forge Silverdale Road.

Silverdale Foundry prior to its demolition in 1998. This site is currently in the process of being developed into a smart business park.

Furnaces

Knutton Forge with the three towering chimneys, Faith, Hope and Charity (third chimney hidden by second).

Silverdale Furnaces

Silverdale Forge 1902

Silverdale Forge

1953 opening of the Belstaff factory with proprietor Harry Grosberg standing to the right of the minister and manageress Mrs Dorothy Whittaker to the left

Charabanc restored by Stan Brunt of Stonewall Estate, who specialised in Rolls Royce repairs. Shortly after this picture was taken the vehicle was transported to New Orleans.